Second Chances

SECOND CHANCES

AT LIFE AND LOVE, WITH HOPE

SHIRLEY RUDBERG GRAYBILL

© 2012 by Shirley Rudberg Graybill. All rights reserved.

WinePress Publishing (PO Box 428, Enumclaw, WA 98022) functions only as book publisher. As such, the ultimate design, content, editorial accuracy, and views expressed or implied in this work are those of the author.

No part of this publication may be reproduced, stored in a retrieval system, or transmitted in any way by any means—electronic, mechanical, photocopy, recording, or otherwise—without the prior permission of the copyright holder, except as provided by USA copyright law.

Unless otherwise noted, all Scriptures are taken from the *Holy Bible, New International Version*®, NIV®. Copyright © 1973, 1978, 1984 by Biblica, Inc.™ Used by permission of Zondervan. All rights reserved worldwide. www.zondervan.com

Scripture references marked KJV are taken from the *King James Version* of the Bible.

Scripture references marked MSG are taken from *The Message*. Copyright © 1993, 1994, 1995, 1996, 2000, 2001, 2002. Used by permission of NavPress Publishing Group.

ISBN 13: 978-1-4141-2134-5
ISBN 10: 1-4141-2134-2
Library of Congress Catalog Card Number: 2011932294

THIS BOOK IS dedicated to my dear children: Todd, Erika, Greg, and Jonathan, and of course my son-in-law Trent, and daughter-in-law, Caytie.

Reading this story may seem odd, for it is a love story of your one parent. Please keep in mind our love for each other never took away from our first loves. The love for your dad or your mom still remains, though we have been separated by death.

Of course, my ultimate love is our Lord Jesus Christ, who gave His life for me—and the best part, was resurrected so that we too will live because of faith in Him.

My hope is that this book will encourage you and your marriages and be a model for you and my grandchildren. I pray we will all have a grand reunion in heaven.

See you at the banquet table!

Contents

Acknowledgments...........................ix

1. Piercing Pain............................1
2. More Troubles..........................11
3. Back to ICU............................17
4. A New Career..........................23
5. Another New Start.....................29
6. I Find a Match.........................31
7. Our First Date.........................33
8. I Say "Yes"............................41
9. Summer Plans.........................47
10. More Graybills........................51
11. Our First Misunderstanding...........55
12. Wedding Day..........................61
13. Our Honeymoon.......................67
14. Mr. and Mrs. Graybill.................71
15. Our New Blended Family..............79
16. Blended Family Traditions............83
17. Honoring Our Late Spouses...........87
18. Other Travels.........................91
19. South Africa..........................95

20. Back Home	107
21. A "Ten"	111
22. Changes	115
23. Without Blair	123
24. Good-bye, Blair Graybill	131
25. Moving Forward	139
26. God Is Good	147
Photos	151
Glossary of Family Members	157
George William Rudberg, Jr.	161
Henry Blair Graybill II	163
Mega-hike is a family memorial for fathers	165
Recipes	167
Endnotes	173

Acknowledgments

My first acknowledgment is to my Lord and Savior, Jesus Christ. Without Him, my life would not have purpose and my years on this earth would lack joy. I would also like to thank my dear sister, Joyce, for her help in editing this book. There are numerous friends who listened to portions and provided ideas. You know who you are. I am also grateful to Christi Krug, my editor, cheerleader, friend.

Chapter 1

Piercing Pain

July, 2005

"How's your headache?" I asked Bill as we sped down the highway. We were returning home from our fantastic fortieth anniversary in the beautiful outdoors when Bill began complaining of a piercing pain in his left eye.

"It's no better than before," Bill shrugged, looking healthy and outdoorsy in his black fleece jacket. "But, I'd rather drive than ride."

I stared out the passenger window, unable to enjoy the scenic beauty of the Idaho Panhandle. Ten years earlier, Bill had been diagnosed with Chronic Lymphocytic Leukemia, known as CLL. Though his oncologist kept it under control with periodic chemotherapy, this pain could be a sign of the disease getting worse. We knew at some point Bill's immune system would break down and something would make him sick. I had a premonition that this might be that "something."

Instead of stopping for the night in southern Alberta as planned, we drove fourteen hours straight home to Vancouver, Washington. When we arrived at home in the early morning, I stretched out aching muscles and helped Bill unpack the car, then flopped onto our bed.

The next morning, Bill's pain persisted despite mega-doses of ibuprofen. "Let's have a doctor look at you," I suggested. Perhaps a stronger prescription could relieve the pain.

As I sat in the crowded waiting room, I thought about our forty years together. The first twenty were difficult. We were two stubborn people, staying together for the sake of our children. I remembered the slam of a door one day when Bill left the family room and got in the car to go on a hike. This was his way of cooling off after an argument. Meanwhile, I just wanted to finish the argument and go on from there. I slumped on the sofa, frustrated that yet again we were arguing over the same things. Later, after Bill came home, he said. "I can't go on like this. What do you think we should do? Get a divorce?"

"Of course we can't get a divorce. We still love each other. What about the kids?" I said, squeezing my hands with the tension. "I agree with you. Something needs to change. We need help."

We decided on counseling, which was a disaster of its own. Re-tilling difficult ground only made things worse. When the last counselor (and we had several) washed his hands of us, he suggested a couples' communication class.

I secretly didn't think *anything* would solve our problem, but we were diligent students. We learned that our stuck marriage was like a scratched record, repeating the same issues over and over. The class facilitator recommended "planned pleasant activities"—dates for the two of us at least once a week. Every week for twelve weeks, we returned to class with six other couples and reported our homework. This would be going out to dinner or coffee or even taking a walk. Our marriage began to flourish. People who didn't know us would never guess we'd had so much trouble.

Now, the hours ticked by at the clinic. The doctor ordered a CT scan, prescribing something for a diagnosis of "cluster headaches." The next day it was back to work for Bill, a manufacturing engineer. Yet even after taking the prescription, Bill felt the burning sensation and had to come home. He tried lying down, relaxing in the family room, even geo-caching —scavenger hunting with clues from the Internet. The nagging pain only got worse. We made several trips those three months to the emergency room during the evening, since daylight brought on excruciating pain.

"Ten being the worst, what would your pain number be?" asked one doctor.

"I don't want to play the numbers game," Bill said in frustration after hearing this question for the umpteenth time. "It's *bad*."

"But sir, that's how we can determine what might be going on." The doctor peered at Bill's forehead, noticing a rash above his left eye, and at last there was a diagnosis: Herpes Zoster Opthalmicus, shingles of the eye.

"Your eye doesn't seem to be damaged at this time," the ophthalmologist announced. "But this will take a long time to heal. Probably months." We thought, *Surely, it won't take that long.*

The rash increased and soon burgundy-colored lesions covered Bill's head like a helmet, spreading from his eye to the back of his scalp. His eye was swollen shut as if he'd been in a fist fight. Though we asked for different analgesics, we were told that nerve pain doesn't respond to most medications. Bill lay in the darkened bedroom, calling out to me with every pain surge. "Ice. Ice!" I would rush to rub an ice pack on his head until the pain subsided and he groaned in relief.

Finally the pain pushed Bill to another trip to the emergency room, where he was admitted to the hospital. An anti-seizure medication seemed to help. Thankfully, Bill's oncologist was at the hospital all week.

"How do you think Bill is doing?" I asked him.

"He has always seemed so vigorous," he answered, "but his color is off. His countenance isn't the same." The doctor's words made me tremble within.

Even Bill's primary physician told us he had never seen a patient whose shingles pain went beyond six months. What was this strange and terrible illness destroying our lives?

Bill couldn't watch television or read a book. Extra noise or movement caused distress. It was terrible to watch my strong mountaineering man so weakened by the virus.

I patted Bill's hand as he sat up in bed. "We have to hold on," I told him.

"I think we can take it a little at a time," he answered. "Let's give it three months."

"Three months," I agreed. It wouldn't be the first time we'd faced a terrifying challenge together. "Remember Rooster Rock?"

Through his pain, he smiled. "How could I forget?"

I thought back to that clear, spring day. The weather was perfect and the Columbia Gorge winds were calm. Bill and I sat on top of the 325-foot monolith, enjoying the view from our perch. The bright blue sky contrasted with the newly sprouted lime-green colored leaves and dark green firs. A soft breeze, smelling of honey from the blossoming fruit trees below, ruffled my hair. All too soon it was time to go back down.

I looked nervously at Bill. Going down meant rappelling off the rock. I dreaded rappelling, though I had forced myself to do it numerous times. If there was a way to walk down off a climb, I would. But it was extremely dangerous to climb down from Rooster Rock, a double-roped cliff, my longest rappel yet.

Bill set up the rope for the rappel down, hooking it carefully into my harness until I was ready to go.

"Just lean back, sweetheart. You'll be OK. Trust me. Trust the rope and protection."

"I can't do this! I'm too scared!" I choked, trying not to cry.

"You *can* do it; I know you can. Put your right hand behind your back and keep the brake on."

I knew Bill's advice was sound. He was fastidiously careful in everything he did. I wanted Bill to be proud of me and knew I had to do it, had to lean back. I had to trust him. I held my breath and tilted backward. *Clunk*! The sound of the chain adjusting itself to the rappel rope gave a jolt. My heart jumped and then I began to ease myself down, talking out loud the whole time. "Okay, okay, honey. I'm doing it. Here I go."

Brake hand back, I reminded myself. *Legs straight to the wall*. I moved one foot down, then the other and eased the rope through the figure eight apparatus. While most climbers will relax and go down quickly, mine was a slow descent. I wanted to get there safely and didn't care how long it took. A few moments later I was at the foot of the rock. I called up to Bill at the top. "Off rope!"

I took the rope out of my harness, waiting for his descent in his black climbing shorts and much-used fuchsia-colored rock shoes. The well-defined muscles of his legs moved with confidence as he rappelled down. He took off his leather gloves and with his large right hand, gave me a high five. "Good job, Shirley! I'm proud of you!" In a playful growl, he added, "You mountain woman, you!" It was his term of endearment, filling me with me a warm glow.

Later, long after we were both down, Bill and I would share that story with others. Bill would relate how he wasn't sure he could convince me to rappel off the rock. He wondered if he'd have to rappel beside me and wasn't sure how he would do that. He didn't realize the power of his persona though, and my need for his approval. The next time I rappelled off Rooster Rock, it was a little easier, though not much. But my encourager was there and that's all that mattered. Now it was my turn to encourage him. As I held his hand in mine, I willed him to feel the love and comfort I had for him.

An elementary school music teacher, I was home for summer break. I drove Bill to his appointments, brought him drinks, fluffed his pillows, played music to soothe him. One morning during devotions, I read James 5:14-16: *Is anyone among you sick? Let them call the elders of the church to pray over them and anoint them with oil in the name of the Lord.* I went into our bedroom where Bill lay and read the passage. "Would you like me to call Paul?" I offered, unsure. Bill rarely expressed a public need for prayer.

Bill gripped my wrist, his hazel eyes earnest. "Call him."

An hour later, two elders, our pastor Paul Jackson, and Bill's good friend, Al, arrived. Bill sat on the couch in his pajamas with a blanket over his legs. I sat beside him, holding his hand, so hopeful. At last there was something we could do. At last Bill could be healed.

Bill talked about his failures. "I've judged others so often in my life," he said, looking up with tears in his eyes. "I've been harsh on people. Many times, I haven't been the best Christian." He shook his head.

I sat with my hand holding his, grateful for the way he was opening his heart. I had to admit it was the truth. After all, I had lived with him for forty years!

He looked at Paul sadly. "I have a hard time with my mouth," he continued. "When I get angry, I say things I know I shouldn't say." There was an accepting silence as the men listened, nodding in compassion. Bill bit his lip. "And sometimes my eyes look where they shouldn't."

"Well, Bill," said Paul. "We all struggle with our eyes, with our mouths, with our thoughts. I'm so glad you can be honest about these things. You are right to confess and can be assured God *will* forgive you."

Bill took his hand from our clasped hands and gestured to me. "I want what she has." I could hardly believe my ears. For so long, I had been praying that my beloved would know the length and breadth of God's love, as I was beginning to know it. And yet, in a burst of anger, Bill would often accuse me of being a terrible Christian. I bowed my head, amazed and grateful for the kind words.

Orville lifted a small bottle. "Don't worry. I won't hurt you." He gently dabbed the oil onto Bill's forehead, careful to find a place without sores.

"Let's pray," Paul said. Bill prayed for forgiveness. Then one of the men prayed for healing. Another prayed for strength. Lastly, one prayed for God's comfort and presence. Afterward, the men stood, each hugged me and reassured me their prayers would continue.

I expected instant physical healing. Instead, I saw a change of a completely different kind. "Shirley," Bill began to tell me daily, "I am so grateful for you." He called his mother. He laughed and listened to Erika, our daughter. I would read aloud to Bill—the Bible, biographies of great Americans, and our favorite author, Chuck Swindoll. We prayed often together. Each time I left the house Bill said, "Drive careful. I need you and love you."

One evening, Bill felt strong enough to meet my mother and two sisters for dinner. As we took our places in the festive Mexican restaurant, Bill greeted his sisters-in-law warmly, then leaned over and kissed my mother on the top of her head. I was surprised at this sweet gesture, for he had not done that before.

Bill was hospitalized at least once in each of the six following months. We grew closer. We were fighting for our marriage, but it was a far different fight than our emotional battle twenty years earlier. This time it was physical. The prospect of one of us losing the other was unthinkable.

It was soon time for me to return to work. But how could I leave Bill? Fellow teachers offered to prepare my classroom and bulletin boards. The principal graciously allowed me to miss several faculty meetings.

Bill was still weak, having trouble remembering his medication doses and feeding himself, even with what little he ate. Most of all, he needed companionship. Willingly, Bill's mom began to visit during the day to make lunch, read to him, and talk about old times.

"I don't want to simply say the blessing," Bill announced at the table, looking from my face to his mom's one night when she stayed for dinner. "I want all three of us to pray together."

Back at school, the beginning of the year was marked with a prayer labyrinth of scriptures and inspirational thoughts. While walking the maze, I picked up a card that read, "Grieving. Please help me stay present to this pain. Support me as I move with it." I was puzzled and scared. What did it mean? What would I grieve?

"I'm really scared," I told my friend Connie, who had been my prayer partner for nearly thirty years.

"What are you scared of?" she asked, leaning toward me through the steam of our coffees.

"I'm afraid Bill will not get better. That the message about grief was somehow prophetic."

"It'll be okay," said Connie, clasping my hand across the table. We bowed our heads. "Lord, help Shirley to be strong. Help her to depend on You to get through this. Help her sense Your presence, no matter what happens."

September 30

Baby Emily Ruthlynn Sagert was born to Erika and Trent. Bill slowly made his way down the hospital corridor. When he took his grandchild in his arms, the lines of pain and weariness lifted from his face. He traced a finger over the downy head. "I haven't missed this moment with any of the grandkids, and I won't miss it now," he said, his voice cracking with emotion.

Over the next few weeks, Bill began taking less pain medication. He emerged from the bedroom during daylight hours to talk with his grandchildren. He grew stronger, went deer hunting with son Todd, and before long returned to work. It seemed our prayers were answered.

We dared to hope that Bill could return to his favorite activities—climbing Mount Hood, (as he had done with his son-in-law, Trent, on one Father's Day), taking his grandchildren clamming, shooting, or dog training, flying Todd's plane, the *Hot to Go*, and enjoying a family outing at Dairy Queen.

One afternoon Bill and I went for a short hike. Bill took huge, satisfying gulps of Pacific Northwest air. An airplane wheeled through the sky. "Looking forward to the day I can fly again!" said Bill, squeezing my shoulder.

In early November, about four months after Bill got sick with the shingles, on a weekend visit with my sister and brother-in-law, Bill asked for medication. "I need it. I'm feeling that pain again! Would you find it for me?"

The nightmare had begun again. Bill couldn't sleep. Nor could I. *Oh, Lord. Please, take this pain away,* I prayed.

The doctors told us that some patients experience "post herpetic pain," though there is no longer a shingles rash. The neurologist prescribed a different medication which came with troubling side effects. Todd jumped in to help, spending hours on the Internet researching drug interactions. Still, there was no solution.

On November 21, our grandson Caleb's fifth birthday, Bill was admitted to the hospital. The hours crawled by. We hardly knew what day it was. Then two familiar faces appeared at the door to the hospital room. "Thought you needed a real holiday meal," grinned Erika, as she and Bill's mom brought in a steaming basket filled with turkey and all the fixings from their Thanksgiving dinner.

On Saturday morning the female hospital chaplain prayed with us and read Scripture. I wept as she read and prayed. "Our Father, please help Bill and Shirley as they cope with this illness. Be their strength and song during this difficult time."

Late that Saturday night, I sat by his bedside while my husband slept. I felt the darkness of the room closing in around me as despair clenched my heart. Then, note by note, I caught the sounds of singing.

Precious Lord, take my hand. Lead me on, through the night. I am tired, I am weak, I am worn; Thro' the storm, thro' the night, Lead me on to the light—Take my hand, precious Lord, lead me home.[1]

The rich alto voice continued to lift old hymns. I stood, amazed, and followed the songs down the hall. A few doors down, I glanced into a darkened room and saw a black woman wearing a black and white dress, sitting in a bedside chair. She would never know the comfort she gave a neighbor that evening. I tiptoed back to Bill's room, knowing I was not alone. Sunday, Bill was sent home with an armload of medications.

A few hours after going to bed one December night, I was awakened by Bill coming into our bedroom. "Honey?"

Illuminated by the hall light behind him, his lean face had a haggard look, and there was fear in his eyes. I sat up with a sudden panic, squinting. "What's wrong?"

CHAPTER 2

MORE TROUBLES

DECEMBER 6, 2005

"I CAN'T SLEEP," Bill said, as he stood in the darkened bedroom. "I feel like I'm going to explode inside. I don't know if I'm going to make it."

My mind was swirling with phone calls I should make, things I could do. Then I saw the image of that woman singing hymns of comfort, her eyes closed, her rich voice filling the sterile hospital halls. I took Bill in my arms. "What a friend we have in Jesus," I began softly, as Bill lay beside me in utter helplessness. Then I began reciting Psalm 23, the way I had memorized it so many years ago. Did *Yea though I walk through the valley of the shadow of death* come before *Thou preparest a table for me in the presence of mine enemies?* I could never remember. Either way, when I peered at Bill next he was breathing evenly, asleep.

"Shirley," he asked, sometime later. "Can you make a recording for me? You know, of those hymns you were singing. And the scripture verses you have been saying. I want to hear them ... in *your* voice."

I looked up while cleaning in the kitchen. "Why ... sure," I said, surprised. But with one thing and another, there never seemed to be a chance to do so.

Yet even in the busyness of caring for my sick husband, I was touched by the help of friends and family. The church sent a crew to clean up the thick fall of fir needles and branches that filled our gutters. A Sunday school teacher brought children to the house, who served cookies and sang Christmas carols. My niece Kelly put up Christmas decorations. My nephew Jonathan drove down from Seattle and offered to detail our vehicle. My sister Eileen trimmed Bill's hair and mustache. Church friends sent encouraging notes.

In our Christmas letter, I included this verse: *Do you not know? Have you not heard? The LORD is the everlasting God, the Creator of the ends of the earth. He will not grow tired or weary, and his understanding no one can fathom. He gives strength to the weary and increases the power of the weak. Even youths grow tired and weary, and young men stumble and fall; but those who hope in the LORD will renew their strength. They will soar on wings like eagles; they will run and not grow weary, they will walk and not be faint* (Isa. 40:28-31).

During Christmas break, sipping coffee one morning, I noticed that one side of Bill's face drooped slightly. With the help of our case manager, we made an appointment with the neurologist for that afternoon, December 23. As we walked out the door, I grabbed *Fill My Cup, Lord,*[2] a devotional book by Emilie Barnes.

The doctor suspected a stroke. As we rode the elevator to the radiation department, I began to read aloud the scripture verses from the devotional book. They strengthened. They comforted. They empowered us to go on.

The CT scan didn't take long and soon we were back in the doctor's office. "Yes, you've had a stroke," he said matter-of-factly. He pointed to the scan. "There's a hole in your brain." Speechless, we looked at each other. At the doctor.

"Is there anything we can do to make his condition better?" I asked.

"Not much at this point...."

"What about the drug that's supposed to reverse stroke symptoms?"

"That isn't useful in Bill's case. With his CLL, that medication is too dangerous."

We walked arm in arm to the car. "I'll never be able to fly solo again," he mumbled. FAA regulations made it illegal for any pilot to fly solo after suffering a stroke.

There was nothing to do but go home.

We applied for long-term disability. After many phone calls, letters, and faxes, at least our financial needs would be taken care of.

January went quickly. I asked for a couple weeks off to be with Bill, who was showing improvement. Maybe, if I could just be with him, this time he would fully recover.

January 24, 2006

I drove to the convalescent home during my lunch hour, gripping the steering wheel tightly. As I walked into the room of my eighty-eight-year-old mother, she held up her arms. "Shirley!" Her voice was quivering and I rushed to her side. She'd broken her hip and was now in recovery. She was small and vulnerable in the stark white bed.

"What's wrong, Mom?"

"They told me I shouldn't bother them by using the call button," she went on. "But I hurt. Why don't they want to help me? Please don't leave me."

I stood there, my heart pounding, my mind whirling. A class of kindergartners was scheduled to enter my classroom in ten minutes. I had no choice but to get back to work. I wanted to crumple into a ball and crawl into bed next to Mom, overwhelmed with all the burdens I was carrying.

"I'm so sorry, Mom," I said.

One evening, we were watching the Vancouver grandchildren and having a snack. Bill's ice cream spoon slipped from his hand and clattered to the floor. On instinct, I knew something wasn't right and flew into action. Erika and Trent picked up the children and I sped Bill to the nearest emergency room. They told us he had a TIA, or "mini-stroke," and sent him home.

The next day, back at work, I was gripped with fear. What if Mom died while I was busy caring for Bill? At the least, Bill and Mom should see each other one last time.

I called home to suggest a visit to Mom. Bill, however, didn't sound like himself. "I'm cold," he said, "so cold." Then he hung up.

As the morning wore on, I worried. I tried calling several times but the line was busy. I rushed home to find Bill putting on gloves, still cold, walking to the truck, ready to meet me.

Since we planned to take two cars to the convalescent center, I drove behind Bill, watching as he swerved slightly, nearly hitting the median in the road. Was this my husband, the excellent driver, who could manage any piece of equipment with ease?

We reached a heavy intersection with eight lanes of traffic, and suddenly Bill swerved again, wildly. I screamed, "Oh God, help him!" My breath caught in my chest as I tagged helplessly behind, while Bill maneuvered the truck like an old man who had forgotten how to drive. Bill clumsily steered into the school parking lot and lurched to a stop. I suggested *I* drive us to the convalescent home. Unlike the man who always insisted on being in control, he agreed.

"Would you like to say goodbye to Mom?" I asked, once in Mom's room. He leaned over the bed and touched her palsied hand as he kissed her cheek. There was a moment of profound tenderness, silence, between these two who had never had anything special in the way of a bond. Now there was an understanding of shared suffering and appreciation. As we returned down the long hallway, Bill leaned on me in near-collapse. Something was very wrong. Another TIA?

"We're going to the hospital," I told him.

Hospital staff immediately began testing for a stroke. The nurse fired questions. As I folded Bill's clothing with shaky hands, I was still weak with the terror of Bill's erratic driving. All I wanted was to sit down and cry, but I had to be strong. I choked out the history of the past six months: the previous night's TIA, the stroke on December 23rd, the shingles, the CLL. I had never realized how being a partner of a sick human being could take such a toll.

The doctor confirmed that Bill had suffered another stroke, more severe this time. As the day passed, Bill gulped down his food in erratic, sloppy bites. He wasn't chewing right; part of his brain was destroyed. My strong mountaineering man could not remember how to chew and swallow. How ironic and cruel!

That night I took a long bath, finally allowing myself to grieve. At last I acknowledged that Bill was not going to get better. I stretched out my limbs in the warm suds, lifting my head to the ceiling of our ranch house, looking beyond to the night sky, searching for God. *Help my husband,* I prayed, *and give me strength.*

The shrill ring of the telephone woke me in the early hours. It was Bill's nurse. "Your husband needs you to be here. Otherwise, I will have to restrain him." I quickly dressed and was soon by his side.

Bill was shifting from side to side, moaning, and yanking at his IV. He pulled his wedding ring off and tossed it across the room. He shivered and stared like a stranger, trapped in his body, unable to control his impulses. I climbed into the bed to hold him. I sang to him, just as before. He rested his head on my shoulder. "Shirrrleee," he slurred.

Sunday morning Mark, a friend and pastor, stopped by his room. "Lord, we pray for Bill," offered Mark. "If it is Your will, please heal him. Above all, we ask that You be glorified out of this illness."

"I am glad Mark came and prayed with us," Bill mumbled in his awkward way of speaking. He choked as he added the words, "Did you notice the last part of the prayer—the part about 'God being glorified'?"

There was silence as we both pondered the meaning. We'd have to let go of our own ideas of this illness. I sat numb, somewhere between panic and tears.

A student nurse stopped in and noticed my anguish. "Come here," she said. With her large, soft body, she took me in her arms and held me tightly. As with the hymn-singing woman, I was once again being visited by an angel of comfort. I knew what she gave me was a hug from God.

Later, Dr. Shanno, the neurologist, explained that all of the main arteries in Bill's brain were clogged. He would need an angioplasty of the brain.

We called Todd in Seattle, who flew the *Hot to Go* down in very poor weather. He reached the hospital while they were performing the surgery. Dr. Shanno's face relaxed into a smile when he came in after the procedure. "It seemed to be successful," he announced. Already, Bill looked better, his eyes alert. He responded to instructions: "Move your leg," and "Squeeze my hand." The doctor fairly yelped after the last directive. "Well *that* works," he said, and we all grinned. Our husband, father, and friend still had his strength.

After two more days in ICU, Bill moved to the regular ward as a good candidate for rehab. "Get better, Dad," said Todd, pulling on his jacket. "I'll see you soon." He hugged his father and left for a work project in Wichita.

I spent Wednesday by Bill's side. My friend, Connie, looked after my mom, whom she called "Aunt Rose." Trent stopped by after work. Erika and our two grandsons, Andrew and Caleb, shared a milkshake with Grandpa. The boys dangled their legs at the edge of his bed as they drank their treat. Soon it was time to leave for the evening. Bill kissed me goodbye. "I love you," he said, returning my hug as I leaned over the bed. "See you tomorrow." He took a deep sigh and added, "I'm so tired."

12:30 A.M. An urgent voice on the phone. "Your husband has had a seizure. Can you come right now?"

CHAPTER 3

BACK TO ICU

"YOUR HUSBAND'S SITUATION is grave," the physician in charge told me. Family and friends quickly gathered, including Todd, who had reached Kansas only to jump back on a plane to Portland. The neurosurgeon from Kaiser looked at the CT scans. Her news was not good.

"I am so sorry. There's been a lot of hemorrhaging. I'm afraid there is extensive brain damage."

We waited. We hoped. Our church elders circled us. I prayed, "Please heal him. Or take him. Don't let me have to choose life or death for him. Please."

"Go home and get some rest," directed the ICU physician. "Your husband is running a fever and we are making him comfortable." He went on to tell us, "The tests have revealed there isn't as much brain damage as we earlier thought."

At home it was scrambled eggs, French bread, and salad for me, Erika, Trent, baby Emily, and Todd.

At midnight, I was awakened. I began to pray for Bill, a voice in my head reciting Psalm 23. This time it flowed perfectly, as though someone were reciting it to me. *The Lord is my shepherd; I shall not want. He maketh me to lie down in green pastures: He leadeth me beside the still waters. He restoreth my soul: He leadeth me in the paths of righteousness for His name's sake. Yea, though I walk through the valley of the shadow of death, I will fear no evil: for Thou art with me; Thy rod and Thy staff they comfort me. Thou preparest a table before me in the presence of mine enemies: Thou anointest my head with oil; my cup runneth over. Surely goodness and mercy shall follow me all the days of my life: and I will dwell in the house of the Lord forever.* (Psa. 23 KJV)

I dropped back to sleep until the phone woke me up at 1:30 A.M. It was Bill's ICU nurse. We needed to come quickly.

He lay there in the dim light with his eyes closed, a tube in his mouth snaking down his windpipe taped securely to his face. I hated that I couldn't kiss his lips. The only sounds were the *hiss, sigh, hiss, sigh,* of the ventilator. The *beep, beep, beep* of the heart monitor. Michael, Bill's nurse, hovered in the background. I sat down beside Bill's bed, feeling the weight of forty years of memories: happy, sad, beautiful, terrible. "I remember the first time I met you," I told him softly. "You seemed so confident, so *old*. After all, you were three years older than me and out of high school. Every time I saw you, my heart would beat a little faster. You were my man!"

I heard Michael chuckle in the background. I went on. "You were always my love. Yes, we had our troubles, but we made it work." I smiled at Bill, squeezing his hand. I searched my heart for scripture, doing all I could to ease fear in Bill's heart. I began quoting Bible verses, infusing my voice with every drop of love and comfort that I could. The nurse had said that the sense of hearing was the last to go. I wanted Bill to hear me now and be comforted.

Distracted by the beeps, I looked up at the monitors, the ever present numbers. "Oh no! Look!" I gasped.

"Don't look at those," Todd gently said in a low voice.

Erika was on the other side of the bed. She choked, "Dad, I love you very much. Thank you for being such a good dad and grandpa. It was so evident you loved my kids. You did it right." She and Todd traded places.

"I'm right here, Dad. I love you...."

Somehow we knew it would be the last time we would talk to him this side of heaven. I glanced around the room, and there was

Paul, our pastor. *Who called him?* I wondered. He nodded to me. I kept my concentration on my dying husband and sang: "Fear not, for I am with you; do not be afraid (see Isa. 41:10). Amazing grace, how sweet the sound that saved a wretch like me."

At 3:00 A.M., I looked at his dear face, strangely gray. Erika noticed it too. And then Michael said, "He's gone." And the family he loved so much had to figure out how to live without his commanding presence.

I don't know how we got home. The world was strange, different, cold. We pulled into the garage, and I drew in a breath sharply. There in the shadows I saw the form of my husband, standing in the corner. I took a second glance. It was only Bill's waders—that wrinkled pair of fishing pants right where they'd been left after a duck hunting expedition one year earlier. *He'll never wear those waders again,* I thought.

"Erika," Todd said, "would you sleep with Mom so she doesn't have to be alone?" He pointed and rattled off instructions. "I'll sleep on the couch and Trent can have the guest bed." I blinked in amazement. He was now the family leader.

I fell asleep, chastising myself in my dreams. *How can I fall asleep when such a terrible thing has happened?* After a few hours, I awoke and heard a robin singing. *The robins are coming back.* And then, it came crushingly back. Bill was gone, never to return. The tears flowed unendingly. I got up in a stupor and began folding laundry, carefully shutting Bill's underwear into drawers. I clung tightly to the red plaid quilted shirt which, no matter how often I washed it, was infused with all the machine smells of Bill's work. I held the cotton to my face and sobbed.

Trent and Erika sat the children down and explained that their Grandpa was now in heaven. Annabel, only twenty months old, of course, didn't understand. Andrew, age six, broke down crying immediately and he and Sarah, Todd's nine-year-old daughter, sobbed and hugged each other. Caleb, age five, was very quiet.

"Eileen, could you go to Costco and buy coffee and dishwasher soap?" I asked my sister. "Also, my piano students need to be notified of cancelled lessons."

Soon, the doorbell rang. A friend delivered a tray of sandwich makings. Minutes later an arrangement of roses landed on the doorstep with a note from co-workers at school. Flowers and food continued to spill inside the house, taking up every available counter space.

My niece Michelle came by with fresh-baked scones. My sister-in-law and niece made phone calls. Everyone helped with tasks, giving purpose to those days of shock.

We met with the funeral director. Picked out a casket. Bought a plot. Chose Scripture. Found musicians. Picked out Bill's clothing for his final rest. Todd adopted his dad's favorite black fleece jacket. "It's like wearing Dad," he said.

Another morning after running errands, Todd and I came home and started up the front steps. Card, the dog, began whining and yipping. "What's wrong with Card?" I wondered aloud. Then as we walked in the front door, we understood. The dog *smelled* Bill on the jacket Todd was wearing. Card thought his master was finally home.

These bittersweet moments were mingled with the comfort of family presence. Erika's family, Todd, and sometimes his daughters, all stayed with me. We would eat, plan, write, cry, share our sleeplessness and memories.

February 7, the day of the memorial and graveside services, dawned clear and cold. As we drove to the country cemetery, I glanced at the familiar place just a short walk from where I grew up. Tucked among towering fir trees, the tombstones dated from the 1800s. I had always felt a sense of peace walking and reading the names and dates, pausing at the grave of my father, other family members, and friends.

We searched for a parking spot in the narrow driveway crammed with cars. I glanced around at Mom Rudberg and Erika with baby Emily in her arms. There were my siblings and their mates, Bill's brother Don and his cousins, and our close friends. We brought Card along, a last-minute decision, so the dog could say goodbye to his master. Cousin Tracy scratched Card's ears while Paul spoke. "Look at the beautiful sky, the birds, the mountains Bill loved to climb," said Paul. In a split second, a plane roared overhead. It was *Hot to Go,* the plane Bill and Todd had spent many months together building.

Its red, white, and blue colors blazing through the sky, the plane flew low over the graveside. In a flawless performance, with a blast of its powerful engine, the pilot spun loop-the-loops, zoomed back overhead, then dipped both wings as if waving goodbye. Then the plane soared out of sight.

At the memorial service we were joined by even more guests. In attendance were Bill's coworkers and bosses from Columbia Machine, the company where he had worked for thirty-five years. Even the CEO had come.

It was a tender moment when Todd stood before the gathering and cleared his throat to read:

> Racing cars and motorcycles, flying an airplane, commercial fishing, hunting, mountaineering and rock climbing—Dad pursued all these activities with vigor. Not only did he pursue them, he was an expert. My dad would share his experiences and knowledge with others by leading them on trips so that they too could enjoy the experience.
>
> Since I graduated from Marine Corps boot camp, I have spent a lot of time and energy trying to make my dad proud. I tried to demonstrate that I was smarter, stronger and more creative than him or anyone else. I may have done a pretty successful job of this neurotic task; I am pretty sure my dad would think I surpassed him. Don't get me wrong, I enjoyed my time with my dad immensely ... especially the last eighteen years. But there was always this underlying theme. In the last week of his life, though, I have come to realize what he desired for me was not what I have worked so hard to deliver. I wish I could have some of those years back. I wish I could tell him that I finally get it.
>
> What was important to my dad was making friends and spending time with them and his family as well as being a productive and responsible member of this church. I have spoken with so many of you who have testified to the positive impact of his life.

While in terrible pain and having suffered the loss of his most dear faculties (ability to hike, to fly, to make love to his wife, for a short while even his ability to speak) he ignored his condition and showed concern for others. I don't ever recall my dad praying out loud that God would heal him, but that God would take care of others around him.

Although fairly quiet about his faith in Christ, my dad ran out of time to lead by example. His son just wasn't getting it. During his last week, never complaining, he purposefully dominated his circumstances to ensure those around him would take notice of his faith in Christ. One of his doctors called me a couple of times to tell me how sorry he was that my dad passed away ... he knew my dad was a special man. The person he wanted to impress the most with his actions? That was me. I am humbled by this man and his sacrifice. I cannot ignore his statement and will endeavor to understand his faith. It is only now that I realize that his finest work was the last twenty years of perfecting his faith and then instructing by example what it takes to be a real man.

Erika followed with her own heartfelt goodbye:

Dad, you were my cheerleader. You invested in me by taking me shopping, out to dinner on my birthday, or sharing a climbing class with me. Just two weeks ago, when we went to the symphony, just you and I, you told me I was beautiful and that Trent was a lucky guy. The most important thing to me now is how you allowed the Lord to complete His work in you during the past six months of your life.

My eyes swam with tears as I shared my own final words for Bill.

"God has truly answered our prayer. You are not suffering any longer, you are with the Father. Oh, my beloved, I'll see you on the other side!"

Chapter 4

A New Career

AS WE SAT around the faculty conference table, I glanced up at the stained black-and-white letters of the sign next to the microwave, which none of us ever actually read: "Your mother is not here, please clean up after yourselves." I brought my wandering mind back to the meeting, where the superintendent frowned, pencil in hand. "There's no easy way to say this. The Board has decided to close this campus at the end of the school year."

Some of us would have positions at the Portland campus. Others, including me, would have to look elsewhere. I was numb to the shock. My coworkers sat frozen in silence. For me, having lost my life partner, this just seemed another thing to lose. Soon, I was applying at numerous private schools to teach music, but was unable to find anything.

My thoughts went to Bill, as they did almost constantly. I thought of how faithful he'd been at Columbia Machine. It occurred to me that maybe I could get a job there amongst his old co-workers. To my relief, there was a position in Production Control and after an extensive interview, I was hired.

This new job was completely different from my teaching career. There were no after-hours sessions, no open houses to attend, no music programs. All I had to do was show up for work every day and leave in the evening. Here, I was walking in Bill's shadow.

My first day I hurried down the stairs to the machine shop, feeling a wobble in my mountain-climber's knees as I passed through Fabrication. What if I couldn't find the right machine? Sure, I had been in the shop before, but I was nervous now. I calmed myself with memories of lunch with Bill, known as George to his co-workers. Machines screeched as I walked through the shop to check on a part and its paperwork. In spite of my ear plugs, I heard the swish of the heat treat oven, the hiss of the welder's torch, the high-pitched whine of the forklift. I could hear snatches of radio talk show hosts, jazz, rock, and, oddly, classical music. The acrid, metal smell laced with the pungent tang of cleaning solvent sharply brought my beloved to mind. Those smells had been absorbed into the very fabric of his clothing. Now, with a pang, I could see him once again in his red plaid, quilted work shirt, coming through the door with a hug for me.

I regretted not appreciating him enough. He had been an artist in his trade. Clean. Respectful. With a positive attitude and a heart full of integrity.

Jodie, a coworker, told me, "I always went to George if I needed something done quickly. He wouldn't gripe or complain about changing a set-up on his machine. He'd just smile and do it."

Although the job became monotonous to him after a time, Bill continued for his family's sake. His work station was always swept clean of metal chips. Now as I walked the aisles of the shop, employees here and there would greet me with respect. Not because of me, but because of *him*. George. I was proud to say I was George's wife.

Working at my computer, I would come across his "fingerprints" in documents, blueprints, and drawings. I would fantasize that, at any moment, Bill would appear around the corner with a cup of coffee or a kiss on the cheek. I mused, how many hundreds of times had he visited this same department?

On all our correspondence, we used the first three letters of our first and last names to notate emails, prints, or drawings. My initials were SHIRUD. Once, checking on a part, I came across GEORUD, right at the bottom. George Rudberg had "touched" this part. It was a drawing of a gear box, a complex, necessary part of the equipment. My heart beat faster as I stared at the computer screen. I gasped and turned to Marilyn, my office mate. "Look what's here!" She came over slowly.

"Wow! Your husband."

"I—I have to go," I said, fleeing for the restroom. I sobbed into my hands as if the grief would never stop. Yet minutes later I returned to work with the sweet lingering confirmation that my dear Bill had been there.

Grief was a strange thing. It had ebb and flow. After Bill had been gone for six months, I still missed him so much! I found a group on the Internet called GriefShare, a Christian organization, and began attending their weekly meetings. I found strength and encouragement through others who had lost loved ones through death.

After attending several sessions, I became a leader myself. This too, bolstered me, while I helped others with recent loss. At the end of a session, I planned a special dinner at my home. I set the table with china and candlelight. Each member brought a reminder of a loved one, a photo, or perhaps a DVD of a memorial service. I gave each person a helium-filled balloon and told her to write a message to the loved one on it. We stood in the cool night air and together released our balloon ships into the starry sky. I watched my own purple balloon rise and pause above the treetops, holding its precious secret. On my balloon, I had written: "You were my first love."

I felt an empty ache. I missed having a mate to share my joys and sorrows. I missed enjoying a meal with a partner. I longed for quiet talks about family and warm loving hugs from a lover.

Yet, in my annual Christmas letter I offered a scripture verse: *Taste and see that the Lord is good; blessed is the one who takes refuge in him* (Psa. 34:8).

My life *was* good. I had family who loved me. Best of all, I had my loving Savior who never let go. My two children included me in many adventures. With Todd and his daughters, Rebekah and

Sarah, I traveled to eastern Alaska to the beautiful Prince of Wales Island. We caught and ate crab, halibut, and salmon and hiked through the Alaskan muskeg. I snapped pictures of Rebekah with her first set of antlers after hunting with her dad.

In late 2007 I went to Florence, Italy, with my two sisters and sister-in-law. We rented a villa, walked narrow cobbled streets, explored nearby cities, and lunched in fine restaurants served by handsome waiters in Armani suits. We were three blondes and one brunette, adventuring, sharing, trading girl talk, playing dominoes.

At times we were taken by fits of giggles, such as when we found ourselves on the wrong train, heading fifty miles *away* from our destination. And once I climbed to the top of the tower of Pisa, peering to the ground far below where my sisters waved joyfully.

On the return flight, I sat between two men. On my right was an engineer returning from Milan. For a time he, coincidentally, had worked at Columbia Machine! On my left, a mountain climber from Seattle swapped stories with me of climbs and sights. After a week with three women, I relished the male conversation. I had missed it. I wanted to meet someone. But how?

"Well, Shirley," said Mom, shifting in her favorite chair and looking intently at me. "If I were looking to meet someone nowadays, I'd do it the modern way."

"The modern way?" I asked.

"Using the computer, of course!"

I smiled. Mom with her spunky ideas was my best advocate. So I joined an Internet dating service, which matched me with Jim. His email said he didn't like writing that much and asked me to call. It turned out he was a pilot, climbed mountains, was a Christian and, like me, enjoyed singing. We planned to meet at a Starbucks and start the new year with our acquaintance. When I arrived, a thin, dark-haired man in a T-shirt was already at the table, drinking coffee. We introduced ourselves and shook hands. I didn't quite know what to do. I was old-fashioned enough to believe he should order my coffee, but as he made no move toward the counter, I took care of it.

"Would you like to get something to eat? Some place quieter?" he asked. So we shared a meal at a neighboring restaurant. Afterward he asked, "May I call you again?"

It was flattering having the attention of a man again, one who had so much in common with Bill. Clearly, from the way he fastened his eyes on me, I appealed to him. "Yes."

"There's just one thing," I told Erika on the phone the next day, "besides the fact there's not a lot of chemistry between us. Jim's divorced. I'm not sure how I feel about that."

There was a moment's silence on the line. "What's your stance on divorce, Mom?"

The patience in her voice made me chuckle. She had heard me many times express my belief that there are few biblical reasons for divorce.

"I guess we both know," I laughed.

"Would you want to compromise your position?" she asked. "Wouldn't it be better to wait and trust God to bring someone who fits your values?"

"Alright, alright!" I said, shaking my head at the way Erika was setting me straight, more like a friend than a daughter. "I'll be patient!"

My job at Columbia paid better than teaching. I met my budget and paid my bills on time. The future looked bright. I planned to stay until retirement age—whatever I judged that age to be. Lately, things were slow at work, which meant I did more part inventory. Numerous times I'd come across GEORUD, and though it didn't shock me as much as the first time, it gave me a twang of longing. Now with the extra inventorying, Bill's initials were popping up again and again, as if they were mocking me. *Stop!* I whispered. Instead of the comfort of Bill's presence, I could feel only loss.

One Friday morning I arrived invigorated by the prospect of a full weekend, having enjoyed spin bicycling class at the gym, time with family, and church. Life was good. From my women's group to my supportive pastor, I had much for which to be grateful. I turned on my computer when my boss, Kellee, called me into her office. The HR manager looked up and nodded. Kellee closed the door.

Twenty minutes later, I heard the speech every employee dreads. I felt as though my world had been crushed. I swallowed my shock, and looked at Kellee. Her eyes were crinkled with concern for me. We'd had so many heart to heart talks about our marriages, Bill's death, our aging mothers. This decision was beyond her control.

The HR manager told me, "COBRA will be there for you for the next eighteen months. You may stay for today, or leave right now."

I couldn't face my co-workers and their sympathy. Kellee walked me out the door and gave me a hug. "I'm so sorry." I would pick up things and clean out my desk later.

The first thing I did after getting in the car was to call my children. I shed a few tears but soon began to remind myself of God's promises. He had supplied my every need during the last six months of Bill's life and had continued to provide every day since his passing.

The comforting scripture came to me. *For your Maker is your husband—the LORD Almighty is his name—the Holy One of Israel is your Redeemer; he is called the God of all the earth* (Isa. 54:5).

Chapter 5

Another New Start

My women's group was supportive about my new job search and wanted to know about my adventures in Internet dating as well. "I haven't met anyone worthwhile," I answered with a sigh. Dorene piped up with a story. Her widowed sister had met a wonderful man on a competing Internet dating service and they were happily married. I politely agreed to try the service, but thought that since I had paid for the full year's subscription, I'd stay where I was.

The next morning, I picked up the phone to Dorene's voice. A mere acquaintance, this was the first time she had called. "I've got to tell you again," she said. "Sign up for the new Internet matching service. You will thank me." I shrugged. When I hung up, though, I thought about it. Maybe God *was* trying to get my attention.

I checked it out, and found they were offering a free three-day trial. There was nothing to lose and everything to gain.

I reviewed my expectations. This man had to be:

1. In the right age range, within a few years of my age
2. Tall enough—no shorties for me!
3. Intelligent
4. Politically active

5. Widowed (though I knew there would be fewer widowers in the pond)
6. A born-again Christian. Not a nominal church-attending man, but one who truly put his trust in Jesus Christ.

I was reminded by my family, friends, and pastor that holding high standards was the right thing to do. If this were God's will in my life, the standards would be no obstacle.

Soon the service started sending matches. Some were interesting but had missing qualifications. They were divorced, lived too far away, or subscribed to a different belief system. Two days passed on my free three days. I began to wonder if, despite all reassurances, my standards really were too high. Then, to my surprise, someone popped up on my matches. A charming, smiling man, he was a father and teacher, two years older than me, conservative in politics, and a Christian. He loved to travel, work out, and listen to jazz. I called my sister Eileen to describe this "find."

"Wink at him," Eileen told me, using the match service jargon. "Wink at him twice!"

So that's what I did. Still he ignored me. *What can I do to get his attention?* I wondered. I took the next brave step and emailed.

> Hi Teacherguy,
>
> I can't believe I'm actually writing to you. Your profile intrigued me because you are a widower. I'm just giving you a little nudge to read my profile.
>
> My best, love2dancein08
>
> P.S. Do you like to dance?

My heart skipped a beat when I received an email with the subject line: "Would you like to dance?"

Chapter 6

I Find a Match

Teacherguy explained that after thirty-two years of marriage, it seemed unreal to enter the dating scene. Yes, he said, he liked to dance, but wasn't very good at it. What was most important to him was his Christian faith; he'd been active in the church many years. "Call me Blair," he finished.

We wrote back and forth with long emails. Blair had been born in Virginia but was raised in Southern California, earned his BA in Political Science from San Jose State in California, then joined the Peace Corps. After earning his teaching credentials, he began his more than thirty-year teaching career. He met his wife while traveling in South Africa. The young family moved to Walla Walla, Washington, where Blair taught junior high English and History and coached football and track.

Blair told how his wife died. I talked about Bill. We circled back to the subject of dancing. "I see marriage as a dance," I said. "In my dancing lessons the instructor explained how the dance is beautiful when the man leads. When the woman tries to lead, both partners start stepping on each other's toes."

Blair chuckled. "I guess both have to do their part."

Our next topic involved "some serious parental bragging," as Blair warned. His oldest, Greg, was a Presbyterian minister and talented writer in Pennsylvania. Greg was married to Caytie, a Pittsburgh girl. Jonathan, the younger son, had a wicked sense of humor and worked at a large bank in Seattle.

In turn, I bragged about Todd, a single dad, software engineer, and former Marine. I told how he and his dad built an airplane together. Then I described Erika, amazing home school mom to Annabel, Emily, Andrew, and Caleb. "We're very close," I said. "We even were blessed to teach at the same campus for three years."

We wrote back and forth, filling each other in. Later Blair told me he had labored over his responses. I, on the other hand, whipped them out as fast as I could type. There was only one fact which nagged at me. He'd had a quadruple bypass fifteen years earlier. Did I want to fall in love with someone with a health problem, who would die and leave me alone again?

Soon we had our exciting first phone conversation, trading thoughts on politics and weekend activities. Then Blair mentioned a local restaurant.

"Applewood happens to be one of my favorites," I told him.

"How about dinner there Friday night? Six?"

So here it was, the big event, our first date. Would there be any chemistry? Would we like each other in person? Though I was sixty-one years old, I felt like a teenager, my stomach full of butterflies.

Meanwhile, I needed something to keep me busy or I'd go crazy dreaming about this guy all the time. It was time for a facelift of my dark family room. I chose a butter color with the ragged look and blonde glaze on top. The week was filled with my continuing job search as well as painting, taping trim, and buying more paint. Yet in every spare moment, I thought of my upcoming date with Blair.

Chapter 7

Our First Date

MY DAY STARTED early Friday morning. I had some paint to touch up in the family room. Yet despite my keeping busy, the day crawled by.

Finally it was time to get ready. I took a calming leisurely bath and styled my hair. I put on black dressy pants and a melon green cashmere sweater to ward off the chill in the air. The stone of my silver necklace picked up the green of the sweater. Glancing at the clock, I noticed time had strangely shifted into high speed. I snatched my purse and ran for the car.

I raced up to the restaurant door and there he was, leaning his shoulder against the building, one knee bent. He straightened and introduced himself. He was as handsome as he looked online—perhaps even more so. Tall at six feet one, he had a full head of silver hair and wore contemporary wire-rimmed glasses that framed his kind looking, hazel eyes. He was sharply dressed in khaki pants with a black checked shirt and a leather jacket in warm brown. We shook hands and smiled at each other as we entered the restaurant.

Our waiter knew Blair as a regular. When our meal arrived, Blair took my hands and unashamedly bowed his head. "Thank you, Heavenly Father, for the food we are about to eat. Thank you for our salvation through Your Son, Jesus Christ. In His name we pray, amen."

We shared lamb chops with garlic mashed potatoes. Blair had a question ready. "Tell me about a meal that was so outstanding you can still remember it."

There had been a special weekend in Ashland, Oregon, thirty years earlier. "My siblings and their spouses met on Labor Day at the Shakespeare Festival. O'Callahan's, near the top of Mount Ashland, served chicken livers. The flavors were exquisite. Since that time," I continued, "I've ordered chicken livers at several restaurants, but they were never quite as tasty."

Blair recounted his enjoyment of a dinner with his late wife and in-laws in a Louisiana restaurant where reservations had to be made a year in advance. The food was fantastic and plentiful.

"So," Blair asked, after a sip of wine. "Do you have plans for tomorrow evening?"

"Wide open," I said, hoping I didn't sound too eager.

"Have you been to Cinetopia?" I shook my head.

He described the unique movie theater with living room style seating where viewers enjoyed movies and good meals at the same time. "Sounds like fun," I agreed.

Finishing our entree, we ordered tiramisu, but only to extend our time together. We talked and talked until it was obvious we were the only patrons in the restaurant. Blair walked me to my car. "Tomorrow evening, then?"

I grinned and nodded.

"I'm looking forward to it." He gave me a sideways hug.

As I reflected on our time together, I realized what was different about him. He was interested in *me*. He didn't need to prove himself by regaling me with information about himself.

Blair met me in the late afternoon sun at the front of the theater the next day. The movie was mediocre, but the man who sat next to me sharing my ottoman was wonderful. As he walked me to the car, this time he didn't give me a sideways hug, but a full-blown arms-around-each-other embrace. I didn't know how long we held each other, but I felt his warmth and caring. When I stepped away, I looked up at him. "That felt good," I said without thinking.

Weeks later, I wondered out loud about my remark. "I'm glad you said that," Blair responded. "If it hadn't been such a public place, I would have kissed you, too!"

The next day, I was floating. Erika sent me a note after church. "I wanted to tell you how beautiful you looked this morning. It was so comforting to walk in and see you singing, and I loved watching you direct Children's Choirs. How thankful we are for you and what you do."

Others too told me how pretty I looked that morning. I knew it was because of a single hug.

Feeling more comfortable with Blair, I invited him to a light dinner. It was Tuesday, his late night at work. I suggested homemade clam chowder with bread and salad. He arrived with an eager smile and a bouquet of flowers.

As I placed the flowers in a vase, he said, "Please excuse me while I visit the loo." I learned that Blair's wife Pat, or as the family called her, Wisha, was English South African and he had picked up many of her charming words.

He opened his arms to hug me and we shared our first passionate kiss. We were both staggered by the emotion. It was as if were we to let go, the other would disappear. "It's been such a long time since I've gotten a kiss like that," he whispered. We both stood, breathless a moment, unable to move. Then we managed to separate to sit at the table.

One of our conversation topics was my job search. I said it didn't matter too much about the salary—only that I needed health benefits. Blair told me later that he had longed to say his next thought out loud: *I have benefits.* Immediately he wanted to offer financial protection.

We spent the remainder of the evening cuddling on the couch, talking and making plans for the weekend. Later that night he wrote, "Shirley, I had a fantastic time tonight. I hope this isn't some kind of a dream. I don't want to wake up and find you gone."

As for me, all I could think about was being with this wonderful man. At our next date, we enjoyed oysters on the half shell, sipped wine, and then stopped to check out a movie—*Shall We Dance*. The movie ended with an intoxicating dance between Richard Gere and Susan Sarandon. Maybe I had found someone to dance my life with, once again.

The next night Blair met my family. I had my visiting grandchildren ready for bed, watching a movie. I was so proud of the boys, aged nine and eight, as they shook Blair's hand like "big boys." Annabel greeted him with a smile and downcast eyes, while Emily was too shy to talk but sat on my lap next to Blair on the sofa. After they had been tucked into bed, Blair and I waited for Erika and Trent while cuddling on the couch. Blair turned to me. "Is it too soon to say I love you?"

"No. Because I love you, too."

It seemed so natural and right. The next morning he asked in an email, "My Dearest Sweetheart, why did I wake up with the world's largest smile? Because I LOVE YOU."

I answered him, "I don't deserve such happiness, but I'm going to grab and enjoy it to its fullest!" I began calling him, "my manly man."

I chatted with my friend Sharon about my new relationship that had grown so quickly. I remembered the fact of Blair's quadruple bypass, and confessed my one fear: losing a partner as I had lost Bill.

Sharon asked me, "Do you want to miss this wonderful relationship because you are afraid? Is it worth it to take a chance? You have to decide."

All right, I told myself. *It's up to me.* Taking a deep breath, I resolved that whatever came next, it was worth the joy of taking a chance with my new love.

On my first visit to Blair's home, a petite blonde woman answered the doorbell, greeting me with a question. "Are you my future sister-in-law?"

I smiled, and without thinking answered with a resounding, "Yes!"

We laughed and continued the conversation inside. "Blair is the prince of the men in this family," Jane told me. "You can't find anyone better." Jokingly, she added, "If he weren't my brother, *I'd marry him!*"

As Blair's youngest sibling and only sister, Jane had been through some tough times, having recently moved from Texas after a messy divorce. Blair had invited her to live with him as she sorted out finances and looked for a job. They were just being family, enjoying each other's company.

That late Sunday afternoon, Blair proudly showed me around the light-filled living room with high ceilings and high arched windows framed with lovely draperies. The furnishings were mixed with antiques as well as comfortable sofas. The floors were tastefully covered with rich oriental rugs, the light honey-colored hardwood glowing in the waning light. He showed me paintings in his living room, some by an acclaimed South African artist and others by Wisha's aunt, with a story behind each. As we walked up the open staircase, he explained pictures of Civil War plantations, replicas of cannons, guns and ammunition, and real cannon balls from West Virginia. "You're passionate about Civil War history," I observed.

"I am. I think it's in my blood."

At dinner, it was fun listening to Blair and Jane spar with each other as we played dominoes. He'd call her a "hussy" and she'd come back with her own pithy remarks. I had my first taste of Amarula, a creamy, sweet South African liqueur made from the marula tree. The taste enveloped my tongue, delicious and indescribable, reminding me of chocolate.

"Ready?" Blair asked as we entered the worship center at Glenwood Community Church. We were holding hands as we walked down the aisle. I'm sure there were curious glances as we walked to my usual place, second row, second seat. *Who's the guy with Shirley?* they must have thought. Normally alone, I was being escorted by a tall, handsome, silver-haired man.

As soon as the service was over, I had my usual responsibilities in the children's choir, so Blair attended class alone. He introduced himself to the Sunday school teacher, Brian Martin.

"Welcome," Brian responded. "Are you a neighbor of Shirley's?"

"No," said Blair. "Actually, I'm dating her."

There was a stunned silence in the classroom. "Well," Brian finally said with a mischievous grin, "I hope you know Shirley has protectors. We'll want to know all about you!" The class broke into laughter. Blair smiled, appreciating how my friends were looking out for me. With every conversation that followed, he quickly disarmed his inquisitors.

To my delight, Blair agreed to join me in dance lessons. For the first time I had my own "real" partner. We were learning the waltz. Though commonly thought of as an "easy" dance, it demands style and finesse, as Kelly explained.

At the dance studio, I hung up my coat, and Blair paused at the coat tree before taking off his jacket. "Will our coats be safe here?"

It seemed strange for him to be nervous. But then, his rich, brown leather jacket might've been new. "Our coats will be fine," I answered.

That first lesson, Kelly was quite hard on Blair. "Keep your back straight!" "No, you've got your hand wrong. Place it on her back, like this!" Feeling sorry for Blair, I looked up at him. He smiled at me, winked one hazel eye and shrugged as if to say, *That's the way it goes.*

We continued with the lesson. The criticisms kept coming. "Not that way!" "Try it again!"

After class, we collected our things. Blair lifted his jacket carefully and put it on, giving the right pocket a pat. I didn't think much about it. I was busy worrying that after the harsh instruction, Blair wouldn't want to go to class anymore. Instead, he grinned at me. "I had a *great* time tonight. That was so fun!"

I couldn't believe my ears. This *was* a mature, manly man. A man who was not afraid to not know everything. A man who could handle not being in control.

Hungry, we stopped for tacos-to-go before heading to my place. Dancing was hard work and really burned the calories!

As I lit candles in the fireplace to set the mood, Blair was surreptitiously putting something behind his back on the couch. I cozied up to him. "Say?" he burst out. "What's this behind my back? It's poking at me." Then he carefully reached behind, beaming as he pulled out a small box. He held it on his palm, presenting it with the question, "Will you marry me?"

My eyes filled with joyous tears.

"You didn't answer my question," he said, "Will you marry me?"

Chapter 8

I Say "Yes"

"YES!"

I didn't hesitate for a moment in answering Blair's marriage proposal. It had only been nine days since we'd first met in person, but it seemed right. We knew what we wanted. We knew this was love and didn't want to waste time playing games or being careful. As mature adults, we had both loved and grieved the loss of our spouses and knew this opportunity might only come once. We discussed many things. How long would we wait to get married? Who should we tell first? Whose church would we attend? "Of course," said Blair, "we'll go to yours." I looked at him in surprise. "You've been there a long time," he explained. "And I'm new at mine."

I had not been this happy since before Bill had died. It was such a delight to be loved and wanted again. Not that my family and friends didn't love me. But this was different. It was love between a man and a woman, so exclusive, so God-ordained, and so right! No more would I wander the house at night, pacing, feeling alone when I couldn't sleep.

I couldn't wait to share with Blair a verse that came to my mind. *For, lo, the winter is past, and the rain is over and gone; the flowers appear on the earth; the time of the singing of birds is come* (SS 2:11-12 KJV). Truly, Blair and I were a fit. Even Kelly the dance instructor had said that our heights made us perfect dance partners. And, he didn't have to bend over to kiss me! My daughter affectionately called us the "cute white-haired couple." We were matched in many interests—politics, faith, travel, music, books. Best of all, we were matched in our hearts. Blair wrote:

> My dearest Shirley,
>
> I was paying some bills with Diana Krall playing, when I was washed over with a feeling of how much I miss you. It seems that each day we grow closer and closer. Are we two lovesick puppies? I know I am. I just wanted to again tell you how much I love you, and how I am looking forward to being together as man and wife.
>
> Love from your
> Manly Man

    The one carat diamond ring, set in gold, fit my finger beautifully, sparkling in the candlelight. "A diamond!" I began. Blair pressed his fingers to my lips. "I know you didn't expect a diamond for your second engagement, but I wanted to show the world how proud I am that you are promised to me, and no other."
    Jane was first to hear the news. The next day, Blair picked up the phone. "Hi Greg, I'm now engaged. Here, meet Shirley!" Then he handed me the phone. We talked awhile and then Blair made the next call to Jonathan. "She's climbed Mount Hood six times!" he boasted. He called his older brother John and his wife, Andy, the couple who had started it all for him, meeting on the same Internet dating service. It was a thrill hearing everyone's excitement.
    Then I eagerly broke the news to Todd, only to hear a long silence on the phone. Todd said, "Listen. I'm really busy the next few months. Why not just go to Hawaii and get married? You don't really me need me there."
    I swallowed, hearing the pain in his voice. Todd had been divorced eight years earlier, and the emotions were still raw. It didn't seem fair that his mom had found the love of her life—twice, while Todd's relationship had ended in brokenness. Even worse, the loss

of Todd's father weighed heavy on his heart. I closed my eyes and said a silent prayer for him.

"Todd," I spoke up, "we want the whole family at our wedding. We want *you* there. You mean so much to me."

I couldn't be sure, but it seemed the hard edge to his voice softened when we said good-bye.

And then Blair and I got mischievous. We didn't tell Erika and Trent we were engaged, but at dinner that evening I wore the diamond.

We were standing around the kitchen, waiting for Erika to place the finishing touches on the aromatic roast pork with caramelized onions, when she looked at my hand. Her eyes widened in surprise. She gasped, "Is that what I think it is?"

Blair and I shot each other a radiant smile. "Yes!" we said together.

We determined to include all our loved ones. We wanted our marriage to affirm the love we had for our beautiful children, grandkids, in-laws, and siblings. This in mind, we arranged for Todd to meet Blair. He had to fly down to a parent-teacher conference for his daughter, Sarah, so we planned dinner in Oregon City.

The van was quiet as Blair and I rode together. I thought of my strained telephone conversation with Todd, and my worries hung in the air. "Here they come!" I said finally, peering out the back window as Todd arrived at the restaurant. He was accompanied by Sarah and Rebekah, with their mother, Kim, at the wheel. As Kim entered the parking lot, she hit a concrete barrier and high-centered the car. Todd and Kim got out, talking together in tense tones. Finally they placed their hands on the rear bumper and gave a tremendous push. The yellow Dodge Neon rocked on the barrier, then there was a scraping sound and a thud as the car slid onto the concrete. Todd stood, out of breath, while Kim was red-faced with embarrassment. What an introduction!

After an awkward silence, I stepped forward. "Blair Graybill, meet my son, Todd Rudberg." In a moment there were shy smiles all around. Blair shook hands warmly and teased, "Well, that's one way to get a parking spot." Over dinner that evening, as we bowed our heads and Blair led us in grace, I felt Todd breathe easier and relax his shoulders. Perhaps he would be able to accept this new man in my life after all.

Later that evening, we took Todd to the airport. On our drive home over the Columbia River, we crossed a bridge, and Blair turned to me with a kiss. "It's our new tradition!" he said. Driving had never been so much fun!

Easter was early that year. "How about a combined family hike?" I suggested.

"Well, I've got an appointment with my trainer on Saturday," he said, rubbing his chin thoughtfully. "But if it's important to you, we can make it work." Again and again, I was amazed by his willingness to drop his plans for me.

At our Easter hike, I finally met Jonathan. I was stunned by the incredible blue eyes of this six-foot, five-inch redhead strolling up my driveway. He had a smile on his face and gave me a big hug. Soon my grandkids were following him around, tickled by his sense of humor and warmth.

The meeting and greeting continued over the next couple of weeks. My sister, Joyce, said after meeting Blair, "There's a sweetness about him."

I continued to be amazed. Blair had an ingenious way of saying things to me. He had such an open, giving spirit.

Hello, Dearest Blair,

I'm going to comment about Greg's sermon now because I will be distracted if I tell you tonight. You know you are quite the distractor! "What Do I Do When I Hurt?" was fantastic. I was intrigued by Greg's section on how God hates (strong word) complaining! I'm sure we've both seen those who do complain and those who don't—how much easier it is to minister to those who aren't complaining. God will reward us for responding rightly to pain. Sometimes, we don't want to discuss rewards or pain or how we respond, but Greg reminds us. What a fine pastor!

I have a wonderful man coming for dinner, so I must close.

Your sweetheart,
Shirley

We made plans to go to Walla Walla, to meet my brother and sister-in-law. There Blair would show me his old stomping grounds: where he taught school and went to church.

Shirley my dearest,

After Wisha died, I didn't think I would be happy again. I was wrong. You are God's gift to me, the product of the forty years you spent with Bill Rudberg. I am lucky to love you and be loved by you. I hope I am worthy of your love! We have chemistry, but just as importantly we are in love with the entire person. If I keep this up, my back is going to arch and I will want to take you in my arms and … I will leave the rest up to you. Do you realize how many bridges there are on the drive to Walla Walla?

Love,
Blair

Needless to say, we enjoyed our trip.

One person remained with whom I needed to share the news. I hadn't been able to reach my pastor, Paul. When he was finally able to return my call, he peppered me with questions. Who was Blair, and what did he believe? What was his family background? How long had we known each other? I nearly talked my voice raw … explaining.

"Okay," Paul finally conceded. "He sounds like a good man. But is there chemistry?"

I laughed. "The chemistry" was the easiest part!

Chapter 9

Summer Plans

Erika, with her amazing organizational skills, put together a wedding notebook planner, laying out my timeline before me. Dance lessons now had a special purpose. Blair and I practiced for our wedding reception, a waltz to "Fascination"[3], by Nat King Cole. Every Friday evening, we would have a private lesson with teachers Tammy and Kelly. Our lessons were intense, yet we also had fun, learning the salsa and the foxtrot.

Blair was reminded to stand up straight and hold his hand on the middle of my back, fingers spread. Our hips were nearly joined together, but our torsos leaned back. My fingers had to be just so on Blair's shoulder. Tammy observed, "As a dance couple, your bodies fit beautifully together."

Kelly agreed, "You're a perfect match."

My biggest job was to follow Blair's lead and all would be well.

One afternoon, watching my youngest granddaughters, I was gazing at a photo. It was a serious shot of Blair, resting his chin on his hand and looking into the camera without smiling. I loved the "come hither" look.

Nearby, Annabel noticed and said. "You love Mr. Graybill, don't you?"

I looked at her little face surrounded by flaxen hair, her gray-blue eyes laced by long dark eyelashes. What an observant four year old!

"Yes, I do love Mr. Graybill." It was obvious to so many—but especially to my own little granddaughter.

Before long it was time for an annual hike initiated by a co-worker in honor and memory of Bill, the Rudberg Memorial Hike. I wasn't sure how the plans would go this spring. Though Blair was in good physical shape, hiking wasn't his thing. When I explained the traditional hike, Blair said, "Of course I'll come. I know how important this is to you." Saturday of Father's Day weekend would be the day.

On the big day, Blair was able to maintain the pace with the rest of the experienced hikers. At one point where the trail crossed a beautiful trickling stream, the two of us stood on a quaint wooden bridge and we shared the moment, engaging in our new tradition.

After the hike, we all stopped at Big River Grill in Stevenson and thoroughly enjoyed a guiltless gourmet hamburger and fries—always the best part of a hard day's hiking. When we got home, it was late and nearly time for bed. I was full of love for my soon-to-be-husband, glad for the way our families were melding.

"I can't sleep," I wrote him. "What better way to tire myself than to write to the man of my dreams? Though I loved my past marriage, I look forward to my marriage to you. It will be different and unique because we are two different people."

The next day, Father's Day, I'd scheduled a garage clean up. My kids were coming to pitch in, as well as Blair, with Jonathan. We were to sort through Bill's tools and climbing equipment. It would be a family project. Yet I knew my kids weren't looking forward to this task. In truth, neither was I. Todd, Erika, and Trent picked through hunting supplies and miscellaneous tools, all hung with Bill's characteristic neatness on pegboards on all of the garage walls. I stayed in the house with the children, Blair and Jonathan.

"Mom," said Todd, stepping inside. "We need to know what you want to do with some things." There, in the middle of the garage floor was a small mountain of items Bill had used in his many hobbies. Todd had selected all the rock climbing gear: hexes, chocks, stoppers of various and sundry sizes, harnesses, chalk bag, and carabiners. When they hung on the wall, it looked like an REI store. He also took the hunting supplies: wet bag, camouflage items, decoys, duck calls, jackets, chest waders. In addition, he knew his father would have wanted him to have his machinist tools in the original chest bought forty years earlier.

A sob caught in my throat as I gazed on the pile. This garage was a symbol of my children's father, and it was being dismantled, as if the last traces of Bill were disappearing. I shook my head, unable to speak.

In the discard pile were a scuffed pair of fuchsia rock-climbing shoes, an image of safety and reassurance. Bill was my climb teacher, reliable and strong. I learned to do elementary moves because of his knowledge and encouragement. And though rappelling and climbing were not what I would have chosen, I did them for *him*—and found strength through learning something new and difficult. Now their owner was gone. Never to return.

It was strangely disorienting to be struck with grief in the middle of a joyous time, preparing for my new life with Blair. But all I could do was face the work before me, knowing God was with me in the grieving as well as in the celebration.

When the garage was finally cleared out, there was a collective sigh of relief. Next, we turned to the kitchen. We sorted tea cups, mixing bowls, dishes, and coffee grinders. My accumulation of forty-two years of keeping house was staring me in the face. It was almost a hindrance. Still, we worked on. Finally, I stood and looked around this old space, its counters bare and shelves empty. It wasn't mine anymore, but someone else's—someone I didn't know. A nameless different person.

Throughout the house, I un-shelved keepsakes, took down pictures, and boxed photographs. Bit by bit, my home was losing its personality. It was as if I and my old life were finally going their separate ways.

Blair and I held a garage sale to reduce our "things." Doing the math, we had housewares from two households with seventy-five combined years of marriage! When the work was done, I collapsed into a dining chair near the bay window at Blair's house. A surge of hope and joy filled me with new energy. This would no longer be Blair's kitchen in Blair's house–but *our* home!

Chapter 10

More Graybills

As Blair and I walked through the Pittsburgh airport terminal, I saw a young man with the Graybill signature look. He was six foot four and good looking, with a cleft in his chin, clear hazel eyes, and a large chest. "Isn't that Greg?" I asked, pointing. He approached and I put out my hand to shake his. But the next thing I knew, he was giving me a big hug. I grinned and hugged him back.

At Greg and Caytie's rural home, we celebrated the Fourth of July. During our week there we lunched in Pittsburgh at a country club, visited a botanical garden, went for a hike, and enjoyed conversation around the table. One morning after Greg prepared Dutch Babies for breakfast, I asked him about his mom. "Did she have a South African accent?"

Greg grinned, jumping up. "Well, I happen to have a recording of it!" He brought out a recording device, which he promptly played. It was the voice of his mother. The voice of Blair's wife, this woman who had played such an amazing role in making him who he was. I teared up. When I looked over, Blair's eyes were also filled with tears. Together we sat, crying to the soft tones of her distinctive accent. She was having a conversation with Jane, and though I don't remember what she said, it was more how she *said* it. It was beautiful. "Her voice was much stronger before the illness," explained Greg. Still, it was *her* voice!

That Sunday, we worshipped at both of Greg's parishes and practiced our wedding dance on the manse's smooth wooden floors. As we listened to Nat King Cole's "You're My Thrill," a joyous rush ran up my spine. The low bass tones on the piano mingled with the high plaintive sighs of the violin, interwoven with the chromatic tones of the haunting melody.

You're my thrill, you do something to me....
Here's my heart on a silver platter[4]

One night of our trip, as I lay awake on Pacific Coast time in the Eastern time zone, Blair padded past my open bedroom door to use the restroom. We both felt an electric longing pass between us. He wiggled his fingers to say hello, but kept walking. I ached to rush out and pull him close. It took all my will power to honor our agreement to sleep in separate rooms until the wedding. That day was less than six weeks away, but it seemed like an eternity.

July 16 took us to the mountains of Colorado for a wedding. As we walked into the reception, Blair pointed out his brother, a trim, dark-haired man named John, with his petite wife, Andy.

"Shirley!" said John, reaching out to me. "I'm so glad to finally meet you!" I was overwhelmed with the friendly welcome, which was repeated by Greg's parents-in-law.

When we finally had a chance for stories, I learned more of Blair's secrets. "I was not only the older brother, but the bigger brother," John explained. "But when Blair was born, our grandfather predicted that one day Blair would be bigger than me." His hazel eyes framed in wire rimmed glasses were full of fun. "But I never believed it, of course." He told how he would bully Blair: most of the time just boyish roughhousing. But there were times Blair felt the roughhousing had gone too far, and he would register a complaint with his parents, which usually yielded a little satisfaction and not much justice. This went on periodically as the boys grew. The problem for John was that Blair appeared to be growing a little faster than he was.

One day during their early teenage years, John began engaging Blair in conflict. "What do you mean, 'conflict?'" piped up Blair. "You were bullying me!"

"All right, all right," John conceded, waving a hand. "This time," he said, continuing, "Blair was as big as me. He stood his ground and swung his fist into my rib cage. I couldn't believe the pain! He knocked me to the ground." Blair had jumped up, furious, charging John, who retreated to the living room for protection from their parents. The conflict ended at that moment and John and Blair had been great pals ever since.

I laughed and sipped my iced tea. "It sounds like you didn't see that one coming."

John agreed. "I didn't. Blair was even-tempered most of the time, and it was always a surprise when he reached his limit. It took a lot to set him off." He told another story, of how, around age five, Blair had gotten angry at something and stormed through the house, face crimson. "There was a stampede of kids in all directions," said John. "They were screaming, 'run! Blair's mad!'"

We all laughed. Blair shook his head, smiling. "Since then," said John, clapping his brother on the back, "Blair has been a very calm fellow."

I reveled in the warmth of the conversation, giddy with love for my fiancé, confident that I knew what I was getting into. By now, I had seen all sides of Blair. I figured there was nothing he could do to surprise or upset me. I was wrong.

Chapter 11

Our First Misunderstanding

WE ARRIVED IN Denver late Thursday evening, after Blair had worked a full day. On Friday we drove for hours on rugged mountain roads, gaining 10,000 feet in elevation. A moose and her calf wandered through the woods and onto the road, and though we were amazed at the beautiful scene, we were too tired to comment. We stared numbly, just wanting to get back to our hotel (an hour's drive to the nearby town) and relax.

We were almost back when we crossed a bridge. In the back seat, Jane leaned forward, her voice teasing. "Blair and Shirley! Time for you know what!"

Blair shook his head and grunted. His face was drawn. "Skip it," he said.

I sat straight with a jolt. What was wrong with my sweetheart? Why was he breaking our tradition? I stared out the window, my eyes filling with tears. I had never seen this side of Blair before. I began to wonder, was it something I said?

The rest of the family, Jonathan, Jane, Greg, and Caytie, decided to go out for fun and conversation at the hotel bar. "I just want to go to my room," Blair said abruptly. This would leave me no choice but to go to *my* room! I was sharing with Jane, and the hotel had moved us to a new room for some reason. I walked the hotel halls, turning, guessing, pointing. None of the rooms looked right. I couldn't remember our room number. That meant Blair had to accompany me back down to the lobby. Blair stood holding our bags while the front desk clerks fielded phone calls and tended to guests at the front of the line. We had to wait a long time. When I glanced over, Blair wasn't smiling. He wouldn't even look at me.

Finally, we went back upstairs with the correct room number. Getting off the elevator, I paused at a door. "Is *this* the right room?" I asked. I still wasn't sure, and the whole thing seemed ridiculously absurd. I burst into giggles.

Blair said nothing, just closed his eyes and opened them again, staring at me as if in disdain. He sighed. This was a new side to my sweet man. My heart sank. Was he not the dream come true I believed him to be?

"Good-night," he said quickly, gave me a peck on the lips, and turned to go. I sat on my bed, disappointed and lonely. What if this irritated, distant man was the *real* Blair? What was I supposed to do?

I unpacked the book I was reading by Dr. Laura, *The Proper Care and Feeding of Husbands* and tried to read. The words were swimming on the pages before my eyes. Finally, I turned out the light and tried to sleep. But sleep, as it often did, eluded me. I tossed and turned all night and finally got up around six, seeking out the closest Starbucks. Around eight, Blair called. "Good morning, sweetheart!" His voice was bright. "Are you ready for another great day together?"

I didn't answer. How should I answer? Here he was, all warmth, after his icy treatment of me the night before. "I'm not so sure," I finally said.

"Let's talk," he coaxed. "Meet me in the lobby?"

I took a seat on the lobby sofa, when Blair came walking up, grinning his old grin. To my surprise, in front of all the lobby guests, Blair knelt down beside the sofa and took my hand. "I am so sorry for my poor attitude last night," he said. "Love is supposed to be kind and I was not. Will you forgive me?"

I blinked at him. "I didn't like being dumped in my room," I said, "without an explanation, without any tenderness."

Blair looked down, his face contrite. "I know. I was tired. I hope that when it happens in the future, we can both collapse together, in the same room, having the other person's understanding."

I felt a small smile form on my lips. Relationships were built on forgiveness. It was just that I'd never needed to forgive Blair for anything before. I realized, he was just as human as anybody else, as human as me.

"Will you forgive me?" he repeated.

What could I do but say yes?

On the plane home from Colorado, I began planning for our big day in earnest. Item by item, we ticked off what we needed to do over the next four weeks. Then, when he was musing over some task, I sneaked my hand up Blair's short sleeve, until I could reach his chest. I tickled the curls there, smiling.

He quietly raised his eyebrows at me, smiling back.

The days were passing quickly. My niece Stephanie Rudberg and her mother Sharon hosted a shower for me. What fun to open presents with my girlfriends and daughter! I received multiple negligees, exactly enough for each day of the honeymoon. I was given a photo album to start Blair's and my life together. It already had our engagement picture. Life was so exciting! Each day in my journal, I would mark off one less day until we were married.

In the midst of my praises, gratitude, and reflections, I would also feel the pang of Bill's loss. It surprised me. "Sadness is only a layer away," I wrote. "Yet in this time, I will enjoy Your blessings, knowing You are with me in the good and bad."

The next Monday it was a hot evening when we went for our dance lesson. We were wearing shorts. Blair gave me giggles in his shorts and leather shoes and tall knee-length socks. "Hey," he said, "these shoes work best for dancing." He shrugged. "Just call me General Montgomery of North Africa."

We were rehearsing at an *un*-air-conditioned church hall and Blair was not dancing as well as he liked. Driving me home, he gave a ragged sigh, staring at the road. "Shirley," he said. "I just don't think I can do it."

I looked up, stunned. I'd never heard him talk about not being able to do anything. He was always positive about himself and others. I laid a hand on his arm. "Yes, sweetheart," I said. "You *can* do it. Even if it isn't perfect it will be fine, for it is *our* wedding dance!"

That night, he went home and memorized the total dance. And on Wednesday before the wedding, we had another lesson. Indeed, he got every step perfect.

The day was nearly here. Greg, Caytie, and Jonathan arrived, as well as cousins. We had a family dinner at Blair's. Together, Blair and I served his signature meal: marinated flank steak, cabbage salad, and oven-browned potatoes. (A true Irishman, he loved his potatoes!) Entertaining together brought us joy. Even cleaning up was a pleasure.

The following days were a whirlwind. With family, we hiked and lunched at Multnomah Falls. There were at-home dinners and games of dominoes. Thursday night before the wedding rehearsal, all family members from both sides went to see a sixties style musical group "The Fabulous Farelanes" at Esther Short Park in Vancouver. It was unusually hot as we sprawled on blankets, digging into our potato chips and chicken while be-bopping to sixties music.

After the concert, a glass of wine in a cool, private restaurant with just the two of us made the perfect "last date" before Blair and I were married.

The next day, Caytie and Jane helped with the table flowers, using the roses, stargazer lilies, and blue hydrangeas offered from friends' gardens. Soon it was time for the rehearsal, and I quickly changed into an outfit just for the occasion. Everyone was there but Todd. He was supposed to fly in from Everett, arrive by two, and pick up his daughters for the rehearsal. He would be escorting me down the aisle for the ceremony tomorrow. *Where was he?*

"Can you call him?" asked Pastor Paul. "We need him before we can start."

Our First Misunderstanding

"I'm on my way," Todd said, when I called. His voice was impatient. "The tux shop had a mix-up with my suit. I think I straightened them out."

When he showed up, Todd looked serious, his brow crinkled. I felt a sinking feeling in my chest. I smoothed my brown and white print sundress, which perfectly matched my snakeskin heels. How could I take joy in these details if my family wasn't happy?

Todd was cool and distant as we continued. He said few words as we followed Paul's instructions. I tried not to worry as we drove to Erika and Trent's place for dinner. Blair and I had our meal and strolled in the backyard, introducing family members. Someone asked Andrew and Caleb about their new step-grandfather. Andrew looked over at Blair, and in his proud voice, announced, "After tomorrow, I'll be calling him Grandpa Blair!"

Rebekah and Sarah were sipping lemonade under the big tree. "Grammie, do you know where Daddy is?" asked Rebekah. I really didn't know. I thought back to when I'd last seen Todd, at the rehearsal.

"He'll be here soon," I assured her, but inside me, I felt the fraying thread of worry.

Finally Todd arrived. "I had to go back to the tux shop," he explained. "They needed to recheck the fitting." He shook hands and talked to guests, seeming okay now. My mixed emotions churned. I wanted so much for Blair's family to see past Todd's unhappiness and recognize what a wonderful young man he was. But I couldn't rush his healing. He missed his dad.

The backyard and living room were still crowded with people as Blair and I said our goodbyes. It would be our last night apart.

Chapter 12

Wedding Day

BLAIR DROPPED ME off that night to a full house. My sister Betsy and her husband, Lyle, were there, and I expected the laughter of Todd and the girls. But I didn't hear their voices. My mind filled with images of dread. A traffic accident. A car breakdown. Worst of all, I feared that Todd had changed his mind and wouldn't show up for the wedding.

I had to calm my nerves. I said a prayer for Todd and the girls, and reminded myself of all the miracles God had done for me. I got ready for bed, knowing I would need a good night's sleep. For some help in that department, I swallowed a sleeping pill.

First thing next morning, Todd and the girls burst through the door with a dozen Krispy Kreme donuts for a treat. "Where were you?" I said, reaching out to give Rebekah and Sarah a hug.

"Your place was full of guests already," Todd said. "I figured a motel would be the easiest choice." He wasn't his happy old self, but at least I knew where he had been.

Todd drove me to the church, stone-faced. As I got out of the car, I turned to him. "Todd, please be happy for me. This is important to me."

"I'll try." His face softened. "I love you, Mom."

It was still early, but I couldn't resist peeking into the groom's room downstairs. My heart pounded. There was Blair! Who'd have thought that even at the age of sixty falling in love could be so overwhelming?

"Sweetheart!" he called. It was a thrill to hear his voice. I was a lovesick girl. "I just want you to know," Blair said, "that I'm very glad we are getting married today. I can't wait until you're my wife. I love you."

"I'm so ready for this too!" I said, squeezing his hand. The warmth of his touch settled my heart. Though the timing had been quick, this marriage was right.

I went upstairs to the bride's room and soon Eileen arrived, ready to put on my makeup and style my hair. I couldn't believe this was happening!

While the photographer, my nephew Rick, was taking photos in the bride's room, Erika and her two girls arrived on the scene. I could hear Emily crying. "Carry me, Mommy! Carry me now!"

Erika groaned. "Maybe having the rehearsal dinner at my house was *not* such a good idea," she muttered, her arms full of wedding supplies. On too-little sleep, Emily was an almost three year old who didn't want to walk up the stairs.

Things smoothed out. Erika fixed the girls' hair. Rick took the opportunity to snap photos of their serious faces. I put my dress on: ivory satin, with a scooped neckline and a back that plunged to the waistline. "Wow!" said Erika. There was a hush around me as I stepped forward, feeling a sudden grace and beauty. I put my hand to my throat and felt Wisha's pearl necklace and earrings, my "something borrowed." Somehow, the cool pearls next to my skin made me feel I had her blessing.

When I arrived in the sanctuary, there was my beloved groom. He had his back turned until the photographer told him to turn around. As he did, he smiled a wonderful, joyful, nervous smile. "You are beautiful!" he whispered. We were soon in each others' arms, if only for a moment.

The time came for all to take their places. Todd took my arm. Erika, matron of honor, was waiting at the front of the church.

Blair stood expectantly with his best men, Greg and Jonathan. All were elegant in their colors of sage and cream, yet I wasn't even conscious of these details planned months before. I clutched my bouquet of plum calla lilies and cream roses, and walked with Todd down the aisle.

My breath was taken away by the sight of so many people. I choked with emotion and pushed the tears back, trying to smile. There was Bob, my former colleague. We had planned many Christmas programs together at school. Oh! There was Earline. Earline and I shared our sad widow times together. Her husband Elvin and my Bill entered heaven nine days apart. There was Sharon, my friend from Columbia. We had shared fun as singles together. There were my family members: Roger, Lexie, Mom; I could hardly contain myself. They were happy tears, though. And then, I was by my groom's side. Paul asked my family if they gave me to Blair Graybill. The answer came, "We do."

Blair took my arm and we walked the stairs to the platform.

Soon we heard the strains of the song, "I've Dreamed of You," sung by my friend Colleen Adent as she accompanied herself on the piano. The song ends with these words:

For God must know how I love you so
He's blessed us here today as man and wife[5]

I gazed into my dear betrothed's eyes. There was a tiny quiver of his chin that I would remember for the rest of my life. How good was God to bring us together!

And then, Paul asked, "Blair Graybill, do you take Shirley Rudberg to be your wedded wife?"

The words resounded throughout the sanctuary: "I DO!"

Paul chuckled at Blair's emphasis. Softly he said, "Thank you, Blair," and the congregation tittered. As for me, my focus was on the man I was exchanging vows with and nothing else. Sometime after the wedding, we would watch the video with surprise and amusement, as the little flower girls, quietly bored, rolled around the sanctuary floor while we said our vows.

Greg who was a groomsman and also a pastor, led communion. He invited the congregation to join in singing "Amazing Grace." As we began, Blair's lips trembled, and he cried. Of course, I cried too. Greg was wiping his eyes. Many tears were being shed—tears of joy.

We signed our wedding license, and Louie Armstrong sang "What a Wonderful World."[6]

Paul pronounced us husband and wife. I thrilled to that long-awaited "kiss-your-bride" command. Blair gave his bride a long, sweet kiss, which seemed enchantingly longer than the ten seconds he had planned.

People stood and clapped as we left the sanctuary. Colleen played "Ode to Joy."

We greeted our well-wishers warmly. When Dorene came through the line, I touched her sleeve and said, "Blair, this is the woman who told me to sign up for our dating service!"

Blair grinned hugely. "I had to wait fourteen months on that service for Shirley to join," he said. He threw his arms around the stunned Dorene. "Thank you!"

We exchanged bites of wedding cake and Jonathan lifted his glass in a toast. "I have to tell a story," he said.

I looked at Blair, who was smiling nervously. He shifted his glass from one hand to the other, watching Jonathan, who was famous for being "earthy" in his language. Was this story going to be off-color?

Jonathan explained how he had attended school in the same district where his father taught. Any time he got in trouble with his teacher, Dad would be informed. One afternoon, after school, he knew Dad would be coming upstairs to discipline him. Jonathan decided to be proactive. He would take protective measures against the expected spanking. He opened his underwear drawer and put on thirteen pairs of "tidy-whities." When Dad arrived and saw he was rather too big around the bottom, he thought better of giving the boy a swat or two. "Jonathan," he said. "I want you to run a mile."

Jonathan continued. "Our place was an acre or so, so Dad told me to run ten times around the back. It was a warm afternoon and with all those layers, that was the longest mile I'd ever run! It taught me not to try and outsmart Dad."

Blair laughed, lifting his glass for the toast. Then Jonathan went on, his tone changing. Sadness crept into his eyes. "I know we've all been through a lot the past three years. I just want to wish you *both,* Dad and *Mom,* the very, very best!"

In my hand, I felt my glass tremble with emotion and gratitude. As we left the church, our well-wishers blew bubbles which gently cascaded to the sidewalk. With a flash, I remembered how disappointed I had been as a nineteen-year-old, when my first wedding ceremony ended. This time, I couldn't wait for our life together to begin. *Here we go!* In the back seat as Eileen chauffeured, we snuggled and kissed some more. Oh, how happy we were.

Our dinner reception was held at a log house that had once been a road house, restored to its original luster. There were toasts by Greg and Erika, Blair's best man and my matron of honor.

Then it was time for the big dance. How would it go? We swirled together, commanding the attention of all our guests. Fashion expert Lexie, my sister-in-law, later commented on my radiant glow. She noted how my dress, the color of candlelight, cascaded as I "moved with confidence to and fro on the dance floor." At the end, Blair tipped me back for another unforgettable kiss.

The reception area was cool enough, but it was still over ninety degrees that evening. Family members from both sides were getting to know each other. Blair's brother, John and our sons, Jonathan and Todd, were all talking flying. Mom gave me warm hugs from her wheel chair. The scene was perfect.

We thought it would be fun to have sparklers lit for our exit, but they showed up as mere plumes of smoke in the still-bright sky. Off we went to Portland's Heathman Hotel. I felt cool and pretty in my black-and-pink-orchids sheath. Blair was wearing khakis and a black checked shirt—a shirt I'd never forget, the one he'd worn on our very first date.

Chapter 13

Our Honeymoon

TOGETHER AT LAST! Six months had seemed excruciatingly long to wait for Blair. I remembered how hard waiting had been for me as a child.

My dad was a pastor and didn't have a large salary. My mom, though well educated, was his helpmeet and his ministry was *their* ministry. There were five of us kids, and each received one gift for Christmas. Mom and Dad had a large closet in their bedroom. "Shirley!" Mom would whisper, and lead me to her bedroom. "Let me show you the doll buggy for Eileen!" I'd ooh and ah, but when my little sister and I were snuggled in bed that night, I'd gleefully tell what her gift was.

"And your present is a doll who walks!" she'd whisper, as soon as she'd had her own visit to the secret closet. It was exciting to find out—initially. But then I had to be just as excited when I actually opened the gift. By that time, some of the joy had worn off. How much better it would have been if we'd waited and *kept* the secret! Thankfully, I learned this lesson as I grew older. Perhaps it was this understanding of joyful surprises that helped me keep my commitment of waiting until marriage for sexual intimacy. And now, just like a gift wrapped in colorful paper and bright ribbons, Blair and I were thrilled with the first-time discovery of each other.

The Heathman was an old and prestigious hotel in downtown Portland, with a lavish wedding suite. There was a chilled bottle of champagne, a cluster of frosted grapes, a book of love sonnets by Elizabeth Barrett Browning, chocolates to nibble, and candles to light. The magic of our honeymoon made everything taste exquisite on this special night. And the sensory delights continued far into the morning hours. The next day as we walked the Portland riverfront in the warm summer rain, we reflected on our wedding day. At a nearby restaurant, we savored a fish entree that we would never be able to duplicate.

Monday morning, it was back to my house to open cards. In lieu of material gifts, we'd asked for charitable contributions in memory of our late spouses.

For Wisha it was the Susan G. Komen Fund. For Bill it was The Leukemia and Lymphoma Society. We opened cards which said "Blair and Shirley" on the envelope, yet also celebrated Patricia Venebles Graybill and G. William Rudberg, Jr. We were cherishing our past, yet treasuring our future.

When we drove to Blair's house later to pick up things for our honeymoon, he unlocked the back door and grinned mischievously at me. Before I knew it, he was picking me up and carrying me over the threshold.

I found a note from Todd:

Mom,

Don't let my wet rag attitude dampen your joy. Although it is difficult for me to show enthusiasm, I am happy for you. There is a huge chasm between emotions and knowledge, and admittedly, I am unhappy with the situation. My Dad and mentor is no longer on earth. I am sure that nobody misses him more than I. Yet I will get used to it.

Blair and his family are honorable and impressive and his qualifications have nothing to do with my poor feelings.

Please give Blair my best congratulations.

I love you, Mom,
Todd

Our Honeymoon

I smiled with tears in my eyes, and shared the sweet words with Blair. We ate one last piece of wedding cake—banana with butter cream filling. Later we drove to my house and spent our last night together in my bed. My old life. Never would I again sleep in this house. When I moved here, I was a thirty-one-year-old wife and mother. There were wonderful memories—such as when Bill got a promotion at work. Memories of conflict, during our highs and lows. Sorrow when we received the phone call that my dad had died. Heartbreak when my nephew Paul took his life at only 29 years of age. Not a large house, yet it was the center for many family gatherings. My children got their driver's licenses while living here. Our daughter's joyous wedding to Trent was celebrated here. Christmases. Dinners. Tears. Arguments. Laughter. Illness. My beloved Bill suffered for many months in this house. And it was in this house that we received the fatal call.

And then, I was there alone. Without my partner and lover. The father and grandfather of my children and grandchildren. The love of my youth. My first love. But then, joy again! In my kitchen, Blair and I shared our first kiss. In my living room, he gave me my engagement ring. We would begin our new life together in Blair's home that was now *our* home!

We had a smooth flight to Hawaii. While waiting for our transfer to Kauai, we shared a meal and I had my first Pina Colada. We were so enthused that, to our embarrassment, we missed our connection and had to wait for a later flight. We stayed in a condo where we had our own private lanai for morning coffee. We read books, moved away from the sun, and cooled ourselves off with a dive into the quiet pool.

Kauai's lazy farmlands reminded me of our own Washington coast. Yet breezes cooled the temperatures, warm water beckoned, and beaches of hot, white sand stretched for miles.

I was shocked to see a gallon of milk cost $10. Wild chickens wandered through the parking lot at WalMart, pecking for worms. We tried a different restaurant every day. We dressed up. I wore my black sheath with orchids to Plantation Gardens, where we shared roast duck spring rolls and thin slices of sourdough bread with butter. We relished tiger shrimp with risotto in cream thyme sauce. For dessert we had Baked Hawaiian—a brownie topped with macadamia nut ice cream surrounded by meringue browned in an oven, splashed with brandy, and lit at the table.

We explored the North Shore where the movie "South Pacific" was filmed. On our way back, we sat on a balcony at Scotty's Ribs, watching the ocean, walkers, and bikers along the promenade while we enjoyed sticky, tender ribs.

Another day, we hiked Waimea Canyon, the largest canyon in the Pacific, ten miles long and a mile wide. In the thick mist, we followed the path, seeing only the blossoms at our sides and the deep red gravel at our feet. When the sun began to burn off the fog, Blair gasped. He was standing at the edge, where the canyon yawned below, a drop of over 3,500 feet.

"Remember, I don't like heights," Blair said in a strained voice, stepping quickly to higher ground. How different he was from my mountain-climbing first husband! And yet I loved him just as much, with all his differences.

I moved in and kissed his cheek. "I know heights can be scary," I said, remembering my Rooster Rock adventure with Bill so long ago. "I'm just glad you're here with me."

"This is more my style," said Blair, the next afternoon, running into the waves with a boogie board. I laughed and followed, the sand warm under my feet. He was right: it was fun! We were playing on the beach near our condo. "It reminds me," said Blair later, out of breath, "of growing up in Manhattan Beach, California, body surfing." And with that he grabbed his board, dipping for a moment as the next wave scooped him up, his platinum hair wet with salt spray.

Chapter 14

Mr. and Mrs. Graybill

"How did you and Wisha get along?" I asked Blair, as we snuggled on the flight home from our honeymoon.

"We didn't have conflicts," he answered. I wondered if their marrying ages made a difference. Bill was twenty-one and I was nineteen, whereas Wisha was twenty-five and Blair twenty-seven when they married.

"But didn't you and Wisha ever fight?" I asked.

"Only once." He explained how they had gone on a shopping trip early in their marriage and apparently he was too "helpful" in the shopping. It was their last and only fight. "From then on," he continued, "I let her make her own decisions about what to buy. We called it a 'command decision.'"

Only one fight in thirty-two years seemed far-fetched. But then I thought about what an agreeable, calm personality Blair had. In our courtship, we'd had only one conflict.

In the coming days, I was curious. "What was Wisha like?" I asked Caytie, Blair's daughter-in-law. I wanted to know better the woman Blair had been married to for so many years.

"She was very organized," said Caytie. "She loved to plan and put things on the calendar much in advance." Caytie admitted with a shrug that this had frustrated her, for she was not a planner herself. I put the question to both boys as well. Jonathan responded that his mom was sometimes a pessimist. This meant Dad would respond to her emotions, wanting to fix the situation when she was unhappy. Yet Blair didn't complain.

I asked the boys once what they thought it would have been like if their dad had passed away first, instead of their mom. They both agreed she would not have handled it well. "It was better the way it happened," said Greg.

One afternoon I was dusting the bedroom, admiring how the rich grain of my old oak dresser matched Blair's oak buffet. They harmonized with the new bedstead and tables we'd purchased, making this our home together.

Yet, when I entered the living room, I gazed up at the large portrait of Blair and Wisha hanging prominently beneath the high ceiling. It was as if Wisha's presence overshadowed my own.

Broaching this subject was tricky. I didn't want to say anything to hurt Blair. I began praying for the right opportunity. Sometime later, after moving furniture around in the bedroom, we were relaxing in the living room and I looked up at the portrait. I was quiet.

"What are you thinking?" Blair asked.

"I'm wondering when you might take down that picture of you and Wisha."

"Right now," he said. He got up, lifted the frame off the wall, and carried it to the closet. In its place, we put a large photo Bill had taken of the Bridge of the Gods at sunset. The deep rose and dark peach skyline perfectly matched the draperies, just as though it had always been there. The bridge stood for our crossing from past to present, from our old lives into new. It would always be the perfect place for us to share a kiss.

This was how we solved our problems. Quickly and without drama.

August 27, 2008

The first day back from our honeymoon, the alarm went off to a Brahms' Sonata on the radio. Blair hopped out of bed.

"No cuddles?" I asked.

"I'm sorry, my sweetheart," he said. "I have to get up—I'll be late for work." An expression of frustration crossed his face as he rushed to start his routine. "This will never do," he told me on his way out.

From that time on, Blair set the alarm twenty minutes early for "cuddle time." It was one of our new routines. The other was daily devotions, a habit that had started with our day of packing and unpacking. I walked down the stairs of our lovely home, a bride of only ten days, and thought, *Is this really my home now? Do I really live here? Am I really married? Did this really happen?*

Blair joined me on the wicker love seat, adjusting the pillows just so and we gazed out at the back yard, feasting our eyes on the end of summer. Pink and purple fuchsias bloomed in their pot alongside the green lawn. Petunias spilled their fresh, spicy scent, and creamy white star gazer lilies bobbed in the breeze with their magenta centers, giving their last push of blooms. We shared our first cup of coffee of the day together. Mine was black French roast, while Blair liked cream and sugar, but was fussy about the cooling effect. To be sure his coffee was hot enough after adding the cream, I tried warming his cup with hot water. You spoil me!" He said, wrapping his hands around the warm mug. It was a sumptuous moment. I looked into my cup of rich dark coffee, the bubbles on top. "And what's little Emily up to now?" asked Blair.

"She's going through a dress-up phase," I said. "Trying on her big sister's clothes."

Blair laughed. "And how did Greg's trip to Pasadena go?" There were prayers to be prayed for our kids. Plans to make. We also talked about mundane things. Did the lawn need to be mowed and fertilized? Should we pull out that dying burning bush?

A moment later we pulled out the devotional. "This one's about the hymn, 'Trust and Obey,'" I said. I tapped my toes and sang for Blair. He smiled. We went on to talk about the passage. I pulled out my prayer notebook. "Today it's the girls' turn for prayer," I told Blair. We each took a turn lifting up Erika and Caytie to their Heavenly Father. We'd begun varying our prayers:

each day we focused on a different child or grandchild. I'd always dreamed of having a devotional time with my husband. At last, it was a reality.

"Dearest, this is an application to Walk with Emmaus," said Blair, leaning over the kitchen counter, next to a small stack of mail. "It is a group Wisha and I belonged to. It would mean so much to me if you could participate in a walk. There's one scheduled for women this fall. Would you be willing to go?" He handed me the application and leaned back, studying my face.

"Well," I said, taken aback. The pages were thick. I paused and thumbed through numerous questions. "Describe your relationship with Christ," said one line. And "please provide an endorsement from your pastor." It looked intimidating. The question was, did I really need it? "I, uh … I've been to many retreats," I finally answered. "I'm not sure I need another right now."

"This is different," said Blair, reaching out and pressing my hand. "It is where my faith in Christ truly began. I'd like you to see for yourself what it's like."

I shook my head, not fully comprehending. Blair went over some of the fine points of his story of faith. At a candlelight service soon after Greg was born, Blair recognized the need for he and his family to attend church together. Yet it wasn't until a few years later, when Blair was in his early thirties, that he realized what Jesus Christ had done for him and made a decision to follow him fully. It was this life-changing event that made such an impact on his spiritual life. "I just want you to see for yourself what finally transformed me," he said.

"If it's that important to you, I'll attend," I said. "But it won't be easy. For one thing, I don't know any of these people. For another, I will miss you!"

"I will miss you too, my love," Blair calmly replied, kissing my cheek, "but I think you will be glad you did this."

"How long is this walk?"

"It starts on Thursday evening, and ends Sunday afternoon."

"That's a long time!"

"Trust me ..." His warm hazel eyes gazing into mine led to more kisses, and it was a long time before we got back to the unopened stack of mail on the counter.

I did trust him, and I filled out the application. Ten weeks after we were married, I would participate in a walk, with Blair the required sponsor. His role as sponsor was to pray for me, and see to it that special notes of encouragement were given at different intervals during the weekend.

We drove to Tri Cities, Washington, after work on a Thursday evening, weaving our way through the streets as twilight fell. "Take a left here," I said, reading the directions. Blair did his best to follow. Two dead ends and a gas station later, we still hadn't found the church. *Good!* I was thinking. *We can go home and I don't have to attend!*

It was dark when we turned into what we thought was a church parking lot. It turned out to be a lawn. I got the giggles—my usual release when nervous, and Blair let out a small sigh of frustration. At last we found the location and Blair hefted my suitcase from the trunk. I would sleep on the floor with at least six women in the converted Sunday school room of a local Methodist church. There were no showers. I handed Blair my cell phone, shrugging my arms in surrender. Reluctantly, I kissed him goodbye.

On our first evening, we were given an introduction and told to begin a period of silence until breakfast. As the walk progressed, I began to understand why Blair wanted me to attend. I relished the wonderful experiences of worship and reflections interspersed with tears of gratitude.

Each day had a special theme. I was impressed with the intense planning and prayer that had gone into the walk. Realizing that Blair and Wisha had been the Director and Directora in years past, I began to respect their role. Many of the leaders in the walk knew both of them. "Shirley, we're so glad Blair found you after his loss," said one leader, Charlotte. Instead of having an awkward time in an unknown city, I had connected with Blair and Wisha's old friends.

Each day I held a note from Blair in my hands, comforted by his large, angular handwriting and loving words. On Saturday Blair returned to stay with old friends in Walla Walla, his adopted hometown. He attended church where the family had been actively involved. Sunday afternoon we had a "closura," a closing worship service, with all the sponsors attending. It was so good to see Blair's smiling face at last as he hurried over to me and we hugged tightly. We talked non-stop on the four-hour drive home. He purposely had not said much about what to expect. Now at last, we freely discussed the different aspects of the weekend and I asked lots of questions.

As the highway rolled on before us, Blair looked over, holding the steering wheel with a jaunty air. "You know something? I don't feel a part of Walla Walla anymore. Vancouver is home now. Home is where you are."

It wasn't the first time that Blair with his gentle, firm personality convinced me to do what he thought was right. He never insisted, but instead reasoned. Before I met Blair, a friend thought I should get kittens to keep me company. My granddaughter's mama cat had a litter and they were convinced I should adopt them. Under some pressure, I did. Linus and Lucy soon became difficult members of my household. They climbed my curtains, sharpened their claws on my couch, and sneaked into closets. I didn't like changing the litter box or finding my favorite silk scarf shredded in their escapades. But what could I do? I was responsible. After all, I had adopted them. One evening, while talking about my new responsibilities with the kittens, Blair said, "Maybe you should find a home for them. It might be better."

I hadn't thought of giving them away. But my daughter Erika really liked tabby cats and Lucy was beautiful, with an extra long tail. Her friend's cat needed a companion, and off went Linus. Soon my problem was taken care of. It was only later in our marriage that Jonathan told me how his dad didn't really like cats. I was astounded. Never once had he mentioned that fact. "But Blair," I asked, "why did you and Wisha have a cat if you didn't like cats?"

He threw up his hands, smiling. "I was outnumbered!"

That fall Blair became a member of my church. Now it was our church. The membership class lasted eight weeks, ending with an acceptance ceremony. During that same evening service, my grandsons Andrew and Caleb were baptized. It was a moving celebration of our blended family.

Chapter 15

Our New Blended Family

As I'd always done, I babysat my grandchildren regularly so their parents could get away. "Do you have the Tribe tonight?" Blair would ask.

"Great!" he said. He'd wait just outside the room while the girls would come in and plop down in Blair's favorite chair. Then Blair would come in with great big steps. "Who's in my chair?" he'd gruff.

Each time they came to our house when Blair was home, it was the ritual. Suppressing a smile, sitting firmly in his chair, the girls laughed impishly. As he came closer, they'd scream in exaggerated fear as he picked them up and tossed them in the air.

Whenever the Tribe came to stay overnight, Blair always had a plan. He thought the meal should be simple and filling. "How about hotdogs and French fries? For breakfast, how about pancakes or waffles—Graybill style?" And, "Let's get a movie everyone would like to watch."

He taught them the importance of table manners. Blair told of the dreaded "bopping spoon." At the dinner table, his father had a long-handled silver spoon. Certain manners were important: using your napkin, keeping elbows off the table, chewing with your mouth closed, and saying "please" and "thank-you." When the Graybill children broke a rule, their father would "bop" them on the head with the spoon. Blair, in turn, used the same method on his boys. They quickly learned proper table manners! Blair never did bop a grandkid, but they laughed at the stories and worked hard to remember the etiquette rules he taught them. At night, before going to sleep, Blair would read *The Bears of Blue River*[7] to the boys.

"Why don't you ever read to us?" the girls asked one evening.

"Well, of course I'll read to you!" said Blair. "But you probably don't want to hear the story of a thirteen-year old boy out in the middle of nowhere."

To the boys he confided, "It's a story my father read to me. I always loved the frontier adventures, not to mention the close encounter with the bear."

After the kids were in bed, Blair and I would spend the dark hours of the early evening paging through photo albums, first one family, then the other. It was as if we were making up for lost time, getting to know these children, the infants they had been, and all the stages in between. There was still much to learn about the other's life and family. On a Rudberg camping trip, I discovered that Blair loved making campfires! That first cool morning in our little tent I asked Blair if he felt like making a fire. He said, "May I?" With delight, he made a teepee-shaped pile of sticks, blowing on coals while I brewed our coffee over the camp stove.

It was important to both of us that we each get to know our siblings. In Arizona, we visited my sisters and their husbands. Blair's sister, Jane, had relocated nearby, and was due for a visit. We played dominoes and relaxed in the sun by the pool at Eileen and Abe's winter home in Phoenix, warmed by the sunshine and the chance to escape the rainy northwest.

We visited Taliesin West, the architect Frank Lloyd Wright's desert home, where architects still learn their trade. A steak dinner, church, football semi-finals—all made for a satisfying weekend.

In February, we visited John and Andy, Blair's brother and sister-in-law in San Diego. Blair and I celebrated our first Valentine's Day at their home. Andy made a special meal to celebrate the holiday of love. I had a special little Valentine gift and card for Blair and presented it to him that Valentine's Day morning. He sheepishly said, "I'm sorry. I didn't have time to get you anything before we left." He continued. "I was too busy."

It was true, our schedules had been hectic. And yet a Valentine's Day without recognition felt like a letdown. "I understand," I said, "but I need you to figure out a way to get some token of recognition. Valentine's Day is very important to me."

After many disappointments on special occasions, I had learned it's best to just tell the guy what you want, rather than hoping he'll read your mind. Most men aren't that sensitive to those special dates and need to be reminded. Blair found a way to get a card for me, and all was well.

We attended John and Andy's church on Sunday morning, and flew to Yuma, Arizona, in their plane. Whenever we traveled together during take off, we'd hold hands. When we landed, another squeeze and we'd give each other a grin of relief. On the ground, safe again.

"I'm amazed at how You worked in my life," I wrote in my journal. "You've answered my prayers, and brought love back in through Blair. I will take this gift and treasure it. I will make him so happy to have married me. I bring him to You as a father, husband, teacher, church member, brother. Please Lord, if it be Your will, give us many years together."

In July, we flew to Manhattan Beach, California, and attended Blair's high school reunion, joined by John and Andy Graybill. We even toured their childhood bungalow, now much changed to a modern, spacious California style.

The longer I knew Blair, the more charmed I was by him. He was a product of his family, all bright and witty conversationalists. As John and Blair reminisced about their childhood days, it was interesting to me that they called their father "Harry," his first name. I asked the two of them why they did so.

John said, "We just always did." They decided it was because their mother called their dad Harry and they copied her. For whatever reason, they weren't directed to call him "Dad." The two younger Graybill children did address their father with the common American "Dad."

At the end of our stay, we shared a burger at the In and Out near the busy Los Angeles Airport and took photos of the descending jets, which seemed to swoop so low they would touch us.

Lord, here I am, on the plane with Blair by my side. Why am I so blessed? It's hard to understand.

Late that summer, my siblings and I rented a house facing the beautiful Oregon coastline in Gold Beach. Each couple took turns making delicious meals. One was "Feul" an Arabic dish made from fava beans, laced with garlic and lemon juice, with pita bread for dipping and jalapeno peppers to spice it further. Peppermint Patties helped to assuage the hot, garlicky taste in our mouths. Another family breakfast was a Quiring family favorite—watermelon and krullers, a German Mennonite specialty. In combination with the sweet watermelon we munched the deep fried pastry that is something like an old-fashioned doughnut without the sugar. We had delicious Northwest salmon for one dinner and Blair and I prepared pasta with gorgonzola and shrimp. For dessert, Blair made one of his favorites, cream puffs filled with whipped cream. We played a lot of dominoes.

CHAPTER 16

BLENDED FAMILY TRADITIONS

IT WAS GOING to be our first big holiday together. Our pastor had been doing a series in the book of Ruth on how God had provided for this widow. When Ruth left her country to follow her mother-in-law, Naomi, to her homeland, she didn't know she would have a second chance at marriage. It was there, gleaning in Boaz's field, that she met the wonderful provider who would become her husband, and their offspring would be the line of King David and ultimately the Lord Jesus Christ. Blair too was a blessed surprise after the huge loss of Bill.

It was with a thankful heart we made our Thanksgiving plans. Blair would prepare a Graybill-style turkey our first year, and the following Thanksgiving, I would prepare a Rudberg turkey. I helped Blair stuff the turkey with sage-thyme dressing. The table overflowed with gourds and fruit, amid sparkling crystal.

With the addition of sister and brother-in-law, Joyce and Dick, niece Michelle with son Joseph, and Trent's parents, there were sixteen around two Thanksgiving tables. We devoured mashed potatoes with turkey gravy and pies of both peanut butter and pumpkin, dolloped with whipped cream. But first we took a moment for sharing. "I'm so thankful for the beloved Boaz God has given me," I said, "in the person of Blair!"

At five the next morning, Erika, Jonathan, and I embarked on our pre-Christmas shopping spree. Jonathan and Erika, new step-siblings, had fun bantering back and forth, like kids. We strategized for our good deals, with one of us standing in line to purchase while the others scrambled for low-priced items. We tracked each other via cell phone.

"How about I make a run to Micky D's for Egg McMuffins?" Jonathan said. "I'll meet you at Fred Meyer." We were home in time for coffee with the rest of the guests.

The days passed quickly. There were Christmas secrets, and smells of wonderful things baking indoors, tempting us. I beribboned the stairway bannisters, so perfect for decorating, wrapping them in green garlands. What would we buy for whom? Blair was a very generous man; we carefully discussed every detail. It was important to Blair that we mail Greg and Caytie's gifts even though we would see them two days after Christmas. Blair gleefully thumbed through catalogues for the "grandies," folding the corners marking pages of potential gifts to be decided upon together. Then came the visit to the tree farm, when the Tribe dashed from one tree to the next. After much excitement and joyous shouts of "there's one!" and "ooh, look at this one!" we found the ten-foot Douglas fir for our high ceiling, fragrant as if it were its own forest right in our home. After tree-trimming and a trip to fill hungry bellies at Wendy's, it was clear how much Blair enjoyed the children—and they him.

I picked through the few sentimental items remaining from my Christmas decorations. Then I opened boxes from the garage. Wisha had collected all sorts of treasures which I explored with excitement.

"You're sure you want all that?" Blair said, watching as I unwrapped the tissue from the snowy old-fashioned Dickens village, the clay crèche, and the Santa and elves display.

"It's like Christmas every day," I said. "Look at this lovely crystal tree!" Later, when Blair came home from work, he touched the snowman display I'd set up on the bureau. "I remember this," he said. "It's lovely."

On the last week of school for Blair and me, snow was predicted. We didn't think much about it as snow rarely stays long in the Pacific Northwest. But late that afternoon, when white snowflakes continued to drop lazily from the gray, leaden sky, we began to believe the weather forecast. It snowed ... and snowed ... and snowed! School was closed for the remainder of the week and we stayed inside, content to watch movies, wrap "prezies,"as Blair called them, and bake cookies, enjoying each other's company.

Weather prevented our family from coming, so Blair and I had Christmas Day to ourselves. The day after Christmas, my nephew Rick navigated the snowy streets to take Blair and me to the airport, where we flew to Denver, meeting Jonathan, Greg, Caytie, and her family. Next we rented an SUV to drive the 100 miles to Frisco, a small community in the heart of the Rocky Mountains. Ski country!

The roads were plowed and dry. "It's not so cold," I said, getting out of the SUV and stretching in the sunshine. I stood at a viewpoint, Blair's arms around my shoulders as we admired the snow-covered peaks. Three minutes later my hands and arms were shivering. "Let's get back in the car!"

"I guess you're not used to zero degrees!" laughed Greg.

This Christmas holiday was a reunion of Blair's sons with their cousins. Wisha's two nieces and their families left summery South Africa to winter in the United States, close to Greg, Caytie, and Jonathan. "Welcome, Shirley! It's so lovely to meet you!" Wisha's niece, Vicky took my hands warmly and, to my embarrassment, I had to lean in to catch every word she said. The South African dialect was charming—but hard to understand.

Ten wonderful days in the beautiful, cold mountains, we played indoors and out, and snow-shoed in a remote valley. It took work and expertise to maneuver the shoes, sometimes plunging off the trail into deep snow, but we became quite good as the day progressed. Mary Caroline Hunt, Caytie's mom, was a good instructor. The sun and clear, crisp air was invigorating, and we lunched near a deserted homesteader's shack.

Warm nights indoors were filled with games and good food, with fifteen of us around the table. The South African family was determined to do a "braai," or barbecue, despite the difficulty of grilling outdoors in zero degree weather with several feet of snow on the deck. I peeled potatoes for Blair as he made his signature dish: marinated flank steak with oven-browned potatoes. Another time I made enchiladas for the entire clan. One day, I made bagels, even with the challenge of baking at a high altitude. Caytie's dad treated us to a sleigh ride drawn by a team of strong mules handled by a "mule skinner." We sailed over the snowy ground to a chuck wagon, where we enjoyed a cowboy meal in a canvas tent, entertained by live country music. As we bundled under warm robes, the clear night sky was glorious with stars.

Chapter 17

Honoring Our Late Spouses

Back home, we were sitting at the table after Sunday brunch when Jonathan leaned back in his chair. "Dad, does Shirley know how much you like football?"

Half an hour later, the house was filled with the sound of the referee's whistle and the crowd's roar. "Tell me more about the game," I coaxed, as Blair put his arm around me on the couch and pointed out the defensive and offensive plays. Andrew and Caleb joined us after church, scooting next to Grandpa Blair.

The Apple Cup, between Washington State University and the University of Washington, was in late November. Blair was a WSU Cougar fan and I a loyal "U-dub" Husky fan. When the Cougs beat the Huskies, he yelled "YEAH!" Then with a guilty look he said, "I'm sorry your team lost." I looked at him, knowing he really didn't mean it. He blinked back at me. "What?" he said, innocently. The razzing and fun added a new dimension to our closeness.

We picked Blair's late night at school as a good time to catch a movie every week. We'd eat something quickly, head off to our movie, and enjoy an involved discussion afterwards. There was still so much to learn about each other.

I soon realized that Blair with his gentlemanly charm had been greatly influenced by Wisha. He referred to sausages and mashed potatoes as "bangers and mash," which made for a hearty "breakie." Chicken thighs were "second joints," and presents were "prezies." If he wanted a nap he would say goodnight to me and the "grandies," visit "the loo," then "get on the bed." I began to develop a great affection for Wisha, looking forward to meeting her in heaven someday. Looking through Blair and Wisha's vast home library, I found many books I'm sure she bought for herself and they were ones I already owned or would be interested in obtaining. I knew that of course I would like her—we both loved the same man very, very much!

Once a year, Blair would drive to the old Walla Walla cemetery where Wisha was buried, surrounded by tall, beautiful trees. Lovingly, he would place a pink rose on her grave. One hot summer's day, we made the drive together.

We visited Bill's grave together too. On Bill's birthday, September 26, we stopped by on our way home from work, arranging a spray of carnations at the gravestone. Blair prayed aloud, "Father, we thank you for Bill Rudberg and the life he lived. Thank you that he is in heaven with You." Joseph Bayly, in his book, *The Last Thing We Talk About: Help and Hope for Those Who Grieve*, about death, wrote this:

> But God is there. He does not despise the decomposing body. It belongs to one whose spirit lives with Him in heaven. Perhaps He sends His angels to guard it until the day of resurrection, as they guarded Jesus' body.
>
> Someday He'll raise it up. He'll raise that body from the dust and unite it once again, part and parcel, indissolubly, with the spirit that made it live, that gave it consciousness and personhood from the womb.[8]

I loved that picture of the angels guarding our loved ones' graves. I loved that each of us honored the first love of the other.

Greg had been working on his book, *Evangelical Free Will, Philipp Melanchthon's Doctrinal Journey on the Origins of Faith*[9] to be published by Oxford Press. When the book was finally ready for print, Blair said, "I'm so proud of him. Let's send congratulations."

Honoring Our Late Spouses

I typed at the keyboard, while Blair dictated. "We are so proud of you, Greg," he began. "Your mom would be very proud, too." At the words, he choked with emotion, his eyes filling with tears. I reached over and threw my arms around Blair. "I understand," I said.

Months earlier, I'd had my own time of sadness. We were driving over Mount Hood, my territory, so I took the wheel. As we neared Government Camp we stopped at the Huckleberry Inn. I was bombarded with images—Bill and me in a booth together, over pie and coffee. Laughing with our climbing group. Stretching our tired limbs. Six times, I had summited Mount Hood with Bill and we always stopped and celebrated. Blair and I ordered a burger and fries to share, and I suddenly became quiet. As we drove south, Three Sisters came in to view. Bill had climbed all three peaks, but we climbed South Sister together. Rugged Mount Washington gave the illusion of being smaller with its pointed peak. That too, we had climbed together. Broken Top and Mount Bachelor appeared in the distance, more summit experiences. To our left was the world premier rock climbing mecca, Smith Rock. We had climbed, hiked, and camped at this glorious spot. I broke my leg there while rock climbing and hiked the gruesome mile out with Bill by my side. Here I had waited for my husband and son to complete climbing Monkey Face, a formidable and daunting rock climb.

It began to grow dark, the high mountain desert seeming to swallow the light. It was hard to see the road, so Blair and I decided not to camp and stopped at a motel in a small town.

As we settled into our room, I was flooded with the heavy sadness of grief. It was an odd paradox. A part of me felt so very, very happy to have my manly man at my side. Yet my throat started to thicken as I smelled the Ponderosa pines of Central Oregon and gazed at the snowy peaks where Bill and I had many adventures. It was my first journey back without Bill. I wasn't going through the area to climb a mountain this time, I was with another man, and though it was wonderful, it would never be the same.

We continued on the next day to a quiet corner of Crater Lake Park. We set up camp, complete with a blow-up queen mattress that nearly filled the tent. Blair set to work building an expert campfire and we sat in the perfect weather, reading our books, eating peanuts from the shell, talking, playing dominoes. The sun moved across our campsite and we moved our chairs to follow it. After a dinner of beef stew, we sat at our campfire in darkness, astounded by the starry sky. The Milky Way was in plain sight, quietly there in the distance. Silent. Big. It seemed we were the only audience.

Chapter 18

Other Travels

In mid-March, we traveled to Yakima, staying at a Victorian mansion. We visited Yakima granddaughters Rebekah and Sarah. My heart was filled with joy to see Blair getting to know his new "grandies." We journeyed on to Lake Chelan, where a social studies conference would begin that afternoon.

Although not a registered attendee, I observed several sessions or sipped coffee in our hotel room overlooking the glassy blue lake. We toured notable, family-owned wineries, tasting Riesling, Pinot Gris, and Sauvignon Blanc, our favorites, and enjoyed the superb reds: Cabernet Sauvignon, Merlot, and Syrah. One winery boasted a wine cave for storing their distinctive Champenoise. Meanwhile, Blair was making plans. "I've got an idea for our first anniversary," he said, "but it's a surprise." Knowing Blair as I did, I knew it would be special—and it was.

We left on Saturday morning in mid-August, just as clear and hot as it had been on our wedding day one year earlier. I thought of past celebrations with Bill, when I had always donned my wedding gown for him. It always made me proud that I could still fit into it and look great in the dress in which I had walked down the aisle. Now, I did the same for Blair, and he gave murmurs and hoots of approval as I descended the staircase in my finery. When I reached the bottom he gave me a fierce hug. "I'm such a lucky guy!"

Cresting the coastal mountains, driving west, I guessed where we were going: the Stephanie Inn at Cannon Beach, Oregon. Our suite overlooked the Pacific Ocean, waves crashing into Haystack Rock that jutted magnificently before us in full view. Our ground floor private patio was decorated with cheery orange reeds and white daisies. Though cool outside, with our gas fireplace on we were toasty, doors wide open as we listened to the pounding surf and smelled the pungent sea air. Scarlet roses decorated our table, alongside a chilled bottle of champagne that we promptly opened and enjoyed with a wedge of Irish cheddar.

In the afternoon we sampled hotel wine offerings with hors d'oeuvres. We walked up the street in the sunshine, cooled by the sea breeze, stopping at Warren House Pub. Like many streets in Cannon Beach, it bore a president's name. Decadent seafood fettuccini filled us until we made the quarter mile walk back to the inn, where warm chocolate chip cookies waited. The weekend was a festival for our taste buds, with night caps and liqueurs, decadent breakfasts of Irish oatmeal, egg dishes, and sausage. On our way out, Blair picked up a creamy nectarine from the large silver bowl. It was sublime.

We shuttled to a downtown beach gallery, falling in love with splashy watercolor posies. We picked up two prints.

"Oh dear," Blair said after some time as we held hands, strolling the sidewalk. "All this shopping is making me weak."

"Really?" I said, lifting an eyebrow at him.

"Maybe," he said, "a visit to a bakery might help."

"Mmm," I said.

"It's all about keeping up one's energy," he added. Needless to say, he perked right up after we split a huge pecan cinnamon roll, washed down with dark French roast coffee.

Blair noticed an antique store behind the bakery. He went inside and asked, "Do you have any frogs?"

"Frogs? Live ones?" the clerk asked, adjusting his glasses.

Blair pointed to a small metal round with spikes, used for arranging flowers. "Oh! Those frogs!" said the clerk, as Blair found what he wanted. I thought it sweet that Blair cared about such details, and the art of flowers.

We walked on the beach, admiring the lovely homes on the bluff, watching people flying their kites in the heavy gusts. Back at the hotel at sunset, we wondered about having a fire on the beach. "Don't worry," said an attendant. "That wind will die down and we'll have a cool evening."

To our surprise, she was right. Too full for s'mores, we stretched out next to the crackling fire and the air felt almost balmy. Before bed we snuggled, watching the DVD of our wedding. One year later, and we were still on our honeymoon.

The next morning, after blueberry pancakes with pepper bacon fried to a crisp perfection, we drove home with contented grins. Some of our commonalities just seemed to grow stronger. Blair enjoyed the fact that I was as interested in politics as he. When he listened to conservative talk shows on the radio during his drive home, he would be pleasantly surprised to find I had been listening to the same program. Even during our honeymoon, we hadn't been able to resist watching the 2008 Democratic convention. Now we watched political programs and raised our voices with agreement or disagreement. We attended rallies together, deciding which candidate we liked. Further, Blair hoped to volunteer for political causes after retiring.

Our next trip was San Francisco, to visit my brother and sister-in-law, Roger and Lexie. We flew to San Francisco on Friday evening where Roger and Lexie picked us up and we went to Rose Pistola for rustic Italian cuisine. After dinner we strolled through the Friday night crowds in the North Beach area and had coffee at Tosca's, where old black-and-white Hollywood photos graced the walls, and it seemed Clark Gable might appear at any time.

Saturday morning we left for the President's Cup at Harding Park. We walked along the fairway, watching Tiger Woods make his tee shot. It was less than perfect evidently, for he frowned as he stepped away, leaving the next stroke to his partner. I luxuriated in the beauty of the golf course, strolling alongside my husband and brother. "Is that who I think it is?" I whispered at one green. Condoleezza Rice, former Secretary of State, was walking with friends, enjoying the tournament as well. Blair pointed out Ernie

Els, the South African playing in the international team. Two months later, we would drive right through Ernie's hometown, George, South Africa, on our road trip through that country.

That evening, Lexie served us a sumptuous meal and we played Mexican train dominoes throughout the evening as Roger and Lexie got to know Blair better.

Sunday morning, we made a hiking pilgrimage to the large cross at the top of Mount Davidson in the center of the City. Lexie told how the Armenian Americans purchased this property when the City planned to take the cross down. We had pizza in Sausalito, took in San Francisco sights on Monday, then flew home. We should've been exhausted. We should've been ready to settle in at home. But we were already preparing for our biggest trip of all.

Chapter 19

South Africa

"WHY ARE YOU taking Shirley to South Africa?" Blair's colleague Ken asked.

"It's like this," he explained. "When my sons have children, they will ask about their late grandmother. I want Shirley to be able to tell about Wisha's homeland."

I smiled to hear this decree. But then I wondered: why wouldn't Blair be the one to tell the grandkids about South Africa? Why was it so important that I learn this information?

As we planned, I asked Blair. "Why don't we take this trip after the school year ends? Then you won't have to take unpaid leave."

"Because I want you to see South Africa during their summer. Besides that, we don't know what's going to happen in the future, and I want us to do this now." He continued, "I've cleared it with everyone at work, and Bonnie will be my long-term sub when I'm gone." In any case, I was delighted with our travel plans. It was to be our second honeymoon, the trip of a lifetime.

"What can I get you to drink?" the flight attendant asked as she handed me a warm towel. I'd never flown first class and marveled at the breakfast offerings: omelets, croissants, ham, sausage, coffee. I squeezed Blair's hand in excitement and he leaned over and gave me a kiss.

At Dulles Airport, I glanced around the South Africa Airlines terminal. Women wore multi-colored headdresses and flowing wraparound robes in yellows and reds which boldly contrasted with their black skin. Languages jumbled in my ears.

We boarded the airbus, then our 17-hour flight in the tourist section began. After a two-hour stop in Dakar, Senegal, it was another eight hours to Joburg. Blair later wrote in his journal, "My bum hurt and no amount of squirming helped. My head bobbed like a doll!"

After the swirl of activity in customs, we were ready to meet our hosts. Blair had described an English-looking couple, and here they came, portly and friendly-faced, walking out-of-breath toward us. "Are they the Adams?" I asked.

"You bet they are!" confirmed Blair. Jen hailed me in her lilting South African accent, Den smiled an enormous smile, and they both hugged me. *That wasn't so bad,* I thought. I had fears Jen might not accept me. After all, I had replaced her deceased sister as Blair's wife.

The hour-long drive gave Jen an opportunity to point out various sites in summertime Johannesburg. There was the Carlton Centre Office Tower at fifty stories high. The Hillbrow Tower was the highest structure in Johannesburg and probably the city's most recognizable landmark which formerly had a revolving restaurant at the top. She told us that the height of the tower is virtually the same as the length of the Titanic—269 meters. She pointed out the Nelson Mandela Bridge. At one of the highest elevations in South Africa, the city is located in the highveld. Half of the world's gold ever produced has been mined from this region.

Den and Jen lived in a high-walled retirement village where palm trees swayed in the breeze and a twenty-four-hour guard secured the gate. They graciously offered us a stay in the second of their two units, complete with bedrooms and bath, a kitchen and "lounge," as they referred to the living room. A brook ran through the complex, spilling into waterfalls, bordered by colorful flowers. Sunset-colored hibiscus blossoms garlanded the wall between our two buildings. Bougainvillea of orange, purple, and red tumbled down the hillsides.

SOUTH AFRICA

First we had a night of erratic sleeping and eating, our body clocks still geared for the Pacific Northwest. Next up was a tour through Johannesburg. The land was dotted with shacks leaning against each other, bordering the freeways. Downtown, we were shocked to see a five-star Holiday Inn completely deserted, while people camped out on the courtyard steps. The sprawling banks and office buildings were empty of people. "It's because of the large influx of refugees," explained Den. Many had left their homelands to find refuge in South Africa. Refugees from Zimbabwe, Angola, and Botswana now filled the cities, while the businesses moved to the suburbs.

"This isn't how it was thirty years ago," said Blair, frowning as he gazed at the city. "We'd go downtown for theater and restaurants. Now it doesn't seem safe."

Once outside the car, we could hear the babble of many tribal languages. We stopped at a shop with a witch doctor in residence. The dark enclosure smelled smoky. There were shrunken heads and dried plants tied together with string and hanging from the dark ceiling as well as shelves of bottles of unrecognizable liquids. People spilled out over the sidewalk. Sellers would stand on an island in the middle of traffic, wares draped over their arms: flags, shirts, perhaps a few apples in their hands.

Our tour of "Joburg" took us to Soweto, the site of the first uprising against apartheid. We toured a museum exhibit of what happened and why. The tour guide was a well-educated, articulate black woman who drove us through the "Beverly Hills of Soweto." Once, Soweto had been the designated area for those of color who were bussed home after a long day's work in Johannesburg. Now, although every home had a pool, it was a scene of ordinary suburban life, with young children walking home from school in their uniforms; boys were in blazers and slacks, girls in pleated skirts and blazers. The guide was hopeful about the changes taking place.

Eager to continue our adventures, we adjusted quickly to the new time zone. Early on Thanksgiving Day, we left for our safari in the bushveld. I was enchanted by the yawningly vast continent.

Insects buzzed and birds cawed. Monkeys chattered, scolding unseen predators.

The guide stopped the Land Rover, quietly bidding us to be silent. I was astonished by the penetrating stillness. Green and brown, the bush reminded me a little of our central Oregon high desert. The bushes and trees were very green, with brown, pointed ant hills everywhere. There were dead trees and we were told the elephants push them over to eat the tender leaves, leaving the trees to die. At the side of the road, in the green bushes, the guide told us to look closely. There, a face slowly came into view, just as in a visual puzzle. A well-camouflaged leopard ignored us, strolling up a tree, stretching out on a limb to take a nap. She straddled the long branch, four legs hanging, long tail stretched out.

"Am I really here?" I whispered, nudging Blair. He smiled.

"I knew you would enjoy this!" he said triumphantly.

Later, on our evening safari, we followed the leopard on a hunt through the bush. Unfortunately, just as everything in Africa is big, so were the rainstorms. We were forced to return to our camp. After the storm passed, we dried off from our drenching, enjoying a gourmet dinner under the stars.

On our second evening outing, we watched an agitated blackbird hovering over a bush. Our ranger and tracker both jumped out to take a look. To their surprise, they nearly stumbled on a ten-foot long black mamba, a deadly snake, and returned quickly to the Land Rover.

On our final outing, we were dazzled by an array of birds and a huge white rhino, his bulk filling the road. Next was a hippo, with enormous round bumps for eyes, his face barely cresting the waterline, belying the huge body.

Onward to Cape Town. We arrived in the middle of afternoon traffic. Kev Adams, Den's brother, was a jovial host, eagerly driving us to Cape Point, Albert and Victoria waterfront, and taking us to dinner. I busily snapped photos from the passenger seat.

And here was another reminder of my Bill: a second Table Mountain. In Cape Town, the Table Mountain summit was nearly

3,600 feet, a substantial climb. "I'm not sure how I'll do," Blair told Kev, "but I want to climb it for Shirley. She loves hiking."

Kev patted our shoulders. "You both can do it, I'm sure of it." The stair-like trail climbed forever. Our clothes were soaked with sweat as we passed people of all ages. The strange thing was, people often dropped water bottles and lunch sacks on the side of the trail, unconcerned about littering. We moved on in the hot sun, with little shade to cool us. Blair wrote later: "One granite step after another. It felt like being on the stair-master for three hours!"

"How are you doing my sweetheart?" I asked him. "Drink. You need water." He would sigh and do as I asked, though exhausted. I would run ahead, snapping photos, returning back down to encourage Blair to keep on.

"This is more like it!" he grinned as we stepped into the cable car for the "climb" down.

We noticed baboons wandering through the parking lot. Signs were posted: "DO NOT FEED THE BABOONS! THEY ARE WILD ANIMALS!" We shook our heads at the strange scene. Later, we hiked up the steep hill to the lighthouse at Cape Point and had lunch overlooking the Atlantic, astounded by the turquoise blue. There I was, touched by the warm breeze, seated in the sun, having conversation with two charming men, one who was my husband. How much better could life be?

On Sunday afternoon we began our trip through wine country and on up the "Garden Route" along the Indian Ocean. My excitement was tempered with nervousness as we drove along the narrow, two lane highway. Blair steered from the right side of the car and I sat on the left. Our car seemed too close to the edge of the road. "Oh, watch out!" I exclaimed as Blair grazed a traffic cone in the city center of Fish Hoeck. Normally not a back seat driver, there were times on this trip that I couldn't keep from saying something.

Blair muttered to himself, "Stay on the left, turn right and go to the far left," as he entered a confusing intersection. In a remote spot, the car in front of us stopped abruptly, and a passenger jumped out and dumped Kentucky Fried Chicken leftovers on the ground beside the road. "How 'bout that?" we said, looking at each other.

We stayed in Franschhoek, wine country, in a centuries-old cottage in the middle of a vineyard. It was decorated in simple country with thick white walls bare of prints. Pine cupboards and simple white couches filled the space, clean and uncomplicated.

"I'm not feeling very well," I spoke up suddenly.

"What's the matter?"

"Upset stomach," I moaned. We stopped for chicken noodle soup at a grocery store. I was concerned about being sick in a strange place with much driving yet to do. "God, please help me recover ... in as short a time as possible." I prayed this, not because I deserved it, but because I could. I had studied James the summer before. *You have not because you ask not.*

After a restful night, despite a storm that rattled the shutters all night long, I felt much better in the morning. We drove through George in the Western Cape. "Ernie Els is the city's native son," I said. "To think we saw him and Tiger Woods just a few weeks ago in San Francisco!"

Our drive along the coastline was sublime. Though we arrived at Plettenberg Bay in the middle of a rainstorm, it didn't last long. Long endless beaches showed off beautiful surf. The soft air shone in a periwinkle, cloud-scattered sky, sometimes called a mackerel sky. Bright blue jellyfish dotted the beach, and a sign warned visitors to beware of their stinging danger. Heedlessly, we strolled leisurely, hand in hand.

After a filling lunch of fish and chips, we stayed in for dinner, each with a book ready. Glancing over I noticed a John Grisham novel. "Are you enjoying your book?" I asked Blair, smirking.

"Um hum."

"Not history this time?"

"I guess you've corrupted me with all your novel reading," he shrugged. Then he looked up, resting the book on the arm of his chair.

"By the way, have I told you today that I love you?" I said.

"And I love you," he answered, giving me a kiss. We sat, snuggling, soaking up the joy of each other's company. "I wonder what people think of us?" I mused out loud. "I'll bet, because of our ages, they imagine we've been married for years and years." Yet we knew we had something special. Not every couple experienced this much pleasure in togetherness.

We spent the next two nights at a private, spacious bed-and-breakfast at Cape St. Francis. We took a walk down a long point, looked at tide pools, and hunted for shells while warmed by the sun. We watched the fishing boats out in the ocean, quite near the shoreline, fishing for calamari. That calamari was the best I've ever tasted.

Next we stayed in Port Alfred. As we drove up to the hotel, the parking lot was swarming with groups of South Africans wearing soccer jerseys, blowing on yellow plastic horns and dancing as a group. A chaotic parade seemed to be forming. We stood by, waiting for a chance to pass, then cut through the bodies, ducking and turning. We reached our room, where a lovely view of the river awaited. But as we looked down, we noticed workers setting up an enormous tent. In a few moments, our lovely view was obscured. "Oh well," I sighed to Blair.

"What else could go wrong here?" he smiled and shrugged. So much for his friend's recommendation of this hotel.

We started down a long hall for lunch only to run into the loud crowd of a hundred, swarming around the buffet. Late that night, reading in bed, we heard a booming, "Testing, 1, 2, 3" in a South African accent, followed by blaring music. Blair pulled on his clothes and marched to the front desk. "Someone is testing a sound system," he complained.

"Sorry, sir," said the clerk, and before long the music subsided. But that wasn't the end of it. Over the next three hours, crowds of loud, drunk guests rattled the walls as they passed our rooms.

We continued our journey along the coast, stopping in Wesley where Wisha's mother had grown up. Blair told me it had been a quaint English-styled village, now turned over to the Ciskei Tribe, who had torn down the houses for firewood. Where once a tennis court and cricket green were carefully tended, there was nothing but rubble. A neat graveyard skirted a white stucco Methodist church. Wisha's family helped finance the upkeep. "Wisha's grandparents are buried there," explained Blair, as we drove along, chuck holes jolting our car.

At Kidd's Beach, Blair remembered a convenience store thereabouts. We stopped at a derelict building, dating from apartheid rule. We walked inside, skirting peeling paint, finding nothing but a few cans of green beans, corn, pork and beans, and a loaf of white bread. "Can we help you?" asked the tired-looking woman at the counter.

Blair asked me quietly, "What do you think?"

I whispered back, "Let's go."

At our B & B, the ocean waves crashed and ebbed. A mother whale and her baby burst out of the surf right before our eyes. "I love being so close to nature," I remarked to the portly, balding man who was our host.

"You might've said different last week," he said. "Bertha, our cat, hunted down a Black Adder and left it in our bathtub!" I had to agree, that was too much nature for me. After that, I was hesitant to enter the shadowy bathroom.

Of the three local churches, we decided to attend the Methodist, the church in which Wisha had grown up. Warm smiles and handshakes brought tears to my eyes. How I'd been missing fellowship with other believers! They reminded me what a beautiful thing it was to be part of the Body of Christ.

We had made arrangements to meet Lu, Wisha's first cousin and her husband Aubrey for lunch after church that Sunday. In her seventies, Lu had red hair, and was a friendly, outgoing woman. She had that same lilting South African accent that was becoming easier for me to understand. They were farmers there in Kaisers Beach. Aubrey was a slightly bald man with ruddy cheeks, who had obviously worked outdoors most of his life. He loved to fish the ocean nearly outside their door, and they ate fresh fish nearly every day. He also loved birds and kept an aviary adjacent to their home. Lu tended a lovely collection of succulent plants in the back yard and the porch was filled with seashells in large bowls. Their children and grandchildren lived nearby.

Off we went to explore the area near Wisha's farm/plantation home. They showed us the local school where a service club had begun working to renovate the buildings. Lu then took us to the pineapple plantation where Wisha's father had farmed for many years.

Blair stood with me on the overgrown grounds, shaking his head. "It's managed by the government now," he sighed. "It used to be so immaculate. There were acres of beautiful flowers." He pointed to the brambles and shrubs. "You can't even see the tennis courts anymore."

He was quiet as we stepped up to the rickety porch and peered through the rooms. Blair took me inside, showing me Wisha's old bedroom. I looked out the window at the frangipani trees, their white flowers putting forth sunny yellow centers. I tried to imagine what it was like for Wisha as a young girl, growing up here. In the yard, I plucked a few frangipani blossoms and breathed in the honeyed fragrance. I placed them in my hair.

"Just like Wisha's wedding," said Wisha's sister, when we saw her. "We wore those same blossoms in our hair."

Our favorite B&B was in a tiny town called Kaiser's Beach, near Kidd's Beach. Our hostess, Dee, had set a hurricane lamp on a worn, chipped table, creating a quaint sitting area on the patio. There, we watched the birds at their bath. Bamboo shades lent an airy feel to our spacious quarters, along with a white comforter and pillows. We slipped out the doors to the garden and beach. I couldn't resist picking up a few sea shells and wrapping them to bring home.

Aubrey was an avid fisherman and met us for dinner with freshly-caught fish chunked and deep fried for a delicious first course. Dee prepared babotie, an Indian dish using springbok, the leggy South African game much like a deer. It was served over rice with condiments of coconut, banana slices, and nuts. Creamy milk tart for dessert completed the meal.

Our second night, Dee prepared a creamy pudding with a delicate crust on top and a rich, warm sauce underneath. With ever a unique flair, she served the dessert in teacups so guests could stand and easily hold them while eating.

Soon we were back in "Joburg." Checking into our hotel, one computer served four desk clerks. Blair looked at his watch. He rolled his eyes and smiled as if to say, *This is not how it would be done in the States.* While Blair and Den waited for our room assignment to check in, I walked around the lobby. The building was like a large mall with the lobby in front. There was a casino along with candy stores, gift shops, and restaurants. Meanwhile, a long line of vacationers dragged their luggage slowly toward the front of the line to be checked in.

The swimming pool seemed the size of an acre. We found lounge chairs with an umbrella to protect Blair's Irish-fair skin. Our waiter was a handsome man with very black skin, dressed in black with a white apron. He spoke with a strong British accent. After he brought our gin and tonics, Blair patted his pockets. "I'm sorry, I don't have any cash with me," he said, signing the hotel check. "Could I leave your tip at the desk?"

There was a pause. "I won't get it if you do," the waiter finally answered politely.

We left, feeling we had cheated a hardworking man his due. Service people depended on their tips—and it didn't take much to please them.

"Next time we'll be prepared," I assured Blair, patting his arm. We wouldn't make that mistake again.

As we were cuddling in bed the next morning, Blair kissed my neck and whispered. "How about room service for breakfast? I don't want to go anywhere."

We lounged away the morning while it rained buckets. Later when the rain stopped, we climbed aboard an all-terrain vehicle for a game safari. Our first encounter was with two enormous hippos hunkering in the distance out of the water. "Hippos have killed more people than most of the Big Five," our ranger informed us.

The "Big Five" animals are: African elephant, black rhinoceros, cape buffalo, lion, and leopard.

Impalas sprang wildly through the bush, their young bounding alongside their mothers. A warthog ran across the road, his comical tail sticking straight up. A kaleidoscope of two dozen giraffes traveled up a ridge, moving as in slow motion.

Again, a moment of wonder. *Was I really here, in South Africa?*

Then we spotted five elephants and a baby. A lone elephant, male and in musk, came walking down the road. He didn't appear to be happy. Shaking his head and fanning his ears, he thundered forward as if about to charge the cars. The drivers backed up their vehicles, and he slowed, finally crossing the road so that we could pass him. The air was full of a musky odor.

Zebras (they pronounced the word, "zehbras") appeared, as well as kudu, an elk-like animal. Rhinos and springbok rounded out our eye-popping safari.

An unexpected opportunity was the on-site casino. Never in my life had I contemplated gambling. My parents taught that gambling and betting were not good things to do. I suppose I even harbored a fear that if I gambled once, I'd never be able to quit.

I remembered many years ago with Bill, walking through the glitz and noise of Lake Tahoe, not the least bit tempted to try my hand at the machines. I didn't like the atmosphere, especially compared to the natural beauty outside.

Now, forty-odd years later, I stood with my new husband in Sun City, South Africa. "What the heck," I said. "I'll give it a try." Investing about ten dollars, I went to the slot machine, doubling my money in about five minutes. "That's it," I said. "Let's collect my winnings."

"You're done?" the surprised cashier said, when I turned in my ticket.

"Yes. I'm done," I continued. "I won. You see, gambling really isn't my thing."

Christmas Day was celebrated with Dave and Vicky, the daughter of Den and Jen. We sat at the outdoor patio sampling ham, roast turkey, potato salad, watermelon, and more. What an interesting Christmas dinner! Yet Blair had rediscovered one of his favorite traditions: plum pudding, a firm, cake-like confection topped with warm brandy sauce and lit with a dancing flame. It was too sweet for my taste, but Blair relished it.

    I came away from my travels delighted, fascinated, sated. Somehow, meeting Wisha's family had made me feel more connected to Blair. I recognized the roots of habits and customs he had taken on over the decades spent with Wisha. "Wisha must have loved you very much to leave her family and country," I told him. I understood how she could love him that much. I did too.

Chapter 20

Back Home

December 31, 2009

OUR FLIGHT HOME from South Africa took place shortly after the infamous "underwear bomber" incident on Christmas Day, 2009. Umar Farouk Abdulmutallab, the Nigerian-student-turned-al-Qaida operative, pleaded guilty to trying to detonate a bomb concealed in his underwear on an Amsterdam-to-Detroit jetliner carrying more than 300 people. The plot was foiled when passengers and crew members overcame him.

Because of heightened security due to that incident only three days earlier, we were not allowed to leave our seats when we stopped for fuel in Dakar. By the time we saw Portland from the airplane windows, we were absolutely thrilled. Snowy rooftops and trees offered wintry beauty, but we shivered, used to our summery vacation climes.

Erika hugged us tightly at the airport, then shuttled us to our home, which she had thoughtfully cleaned and warmed. Even the refrigerator was stocked, so that when we awoke in the early hours, our jet-lagged bodies expecting lunch, we'd have something to eat. We celebrated the New Year by going to bed at nine P.M.

Blair had missed nearly six weeks of football, so catching up was a serious business. Football games consumed Saturday and

Sunday, while Blair, no couch potato, laid out files and folders on the couch and tables. "It's a good time to organize our financial files," he said.

"When do you think we'll finish combining everything?" I asked, looking at the sea of paper. We were still tying up loose ends of our previous marriages, and reviewing important documents such as our wills.

"I don't know," shrugged Blair. "But there's no hurry. We have plenty of time."

I picked up a document and turned the pages. "You'll be buried next to Wisha, it says here, at the plot in Walla Walla," I mused. It wasn't news to me, but there were details we needed to clarify.

"My name is already on the headstone," said Blair, not looking up.

"Yes. And your wedding date. December ... what was it?"

"December 23, 1972," said Blair, leaning back on the couch pillows. I stood by, holding out the pages of the document.

Blair glanced at me, then bit his lip, then with resolution reached over and clicked off the television. "It has already been decided," he said. "You'll be buried next to Bill. I'll be with Wisha."

Our voices were low, serious. There was tension in the bright room. A starry night sky showed through the high windows.

"I know," I said carefully. "I understand why you need to be buried next to her. You're keeping your promise to Wisha. But I feel left out. What about *our* marriage? Is that to go unmentioned?"

Carefully, reasonably, we continued our discussion, keeping our voices level, doing our best to state our points of view and listen to the other. "We do need to acknowledge that we had children with our first mates," said Blair, folding his hands together. "It makes sense that we should honor that union."

"Yes," I agreed, dropping onto the couch next to him. "But shouldn't we include our own marriage covenant?"

Blair tilted his head to the side thoughtfully. "Yes," he said. "But how?"

As we talked, we came up with a plan. Blair's headstone would include the following: "Married Shirley Mae Rudberg on August 16, 2008." My headstone hadn't been placed nor purchased, but it would have my newest last name: Graybill.

"I would be honored to have your name at my final resting place," said Blair, and gently reached out and squeezed my hand. I smiled with relief, my tension eased.

"Will you be playing for the community orchestra concert?" asked Blair. I'd missed more than a month of violin rehearsals while traveling.

"I'm going to try," I said, lifting my chin. "After all, you're the only person I would want to impress."

"Then I'm sure you'll be fine," said Blair, kissing my cheek.

Soon it was the night of our Portland performance. Beforehand, as was usual, we tuned our instruments and straightened our music. Once the conductor's baton came down, there would be no glancing around, so I craned my neck from the orchestra pit, my eyes searching for the one person I cared most about in the audience. I couldn't find him anywhere!

A wave of fear and loneliness swept over me. But then I saw the silver hair, the bright smile, the hazel eyes aimed right at me. It was as if he read my thoughts. I felt centered, calmed. I played confidently.

"You were wonderful, my sweetheart," Blair said after the concert. I breathed a prayer of gratitude. In such a short time, this man had become an integral part of everything I did.

January's calendar filled with more weekend concerts, a trip to Sandy, Oregon, and even a belated Christmas party with Erika and Todd. Being a fun-loving gal, I was always ready for a gathering. "How about a Super Bowl party?" I suggested.

Blair looked askance. "If we have people over, will we still watch football?"

"Of course!"

He peered at me skeptically. "You're sure. No socializing during the game?"

I smiled and nodded. We imagined the party. Trent and Erika would bring the Tribe, and of course we'd invite Connie and Mac Storey. Andrew would cheer for the Saints, while young Caleb would no doubt sit near Grandpa Blair as they rooted together for their team, the Colts.

Blair stood up and marked the kitchen calendar. "Sounds like fun."

"I'll make the phone calls," I said.

Was it only two years ago we'd met? It seemed like a lifetime. We planned to have dinner at Applewood, on February 8th, where we had our first date.

We were reliving our South Africa memories as well. Blair gave a slide show series for his co-workers, narrating our travels. When he came home he said, "I love you very, very, very, very much!" Each time he said "very" he kissed me and smiled with delight. We laughed and fell into each other's arms.

One evening was particularly busy. I'd promised to attend a friend's art exhibit, followed by worship team rehearsal at church. I left Blair a note about dinner on the stove, adding, "I love, love, love YOU!"

Afterward, I slipped into the bedroom quietly, thinking he was asleep. "How was the exhibit?" Blair asked, sitting up.

"Well-attended," I said. "And very good. Alex did a nice job." I unwrapped my scarf and laid it on the dresser. "And how was your day?"

"Busy. Enough time to grade papers, though," he continued. "I showed the second disk of our trip—everyone loved it."

"Great," I said. "So what's next on our agenda?"

"Jonathan's birthday," said Blair.

"This Saturday," I noted. "He'll be thirty-two."

"I've got his gift ordered from Amazon" added Blair. "He asked for that game for his Playstation. Will you sign the card?" I nodded. "Say," Blair continued, "we need to get back to our workouts."

"Sounds good," I agreed, stepping into my slippers.

"I'll see if I can get an appointment with Chris after work," he finished.

"Thanks," I said, reaching for my toothbrush. It was wonderful to be a team, in our exercise routine, in little things and in big.

Oh, such plans we had.

Chapter 21

A "Ten"

January 29, 2010

THE STRAINS OF Brahms broke the early morning silence. Blair hit the snooze alarm and it was time to snuggle. Blair put his arm around me and I put my ear on his chest, hearing the steady rhythm of his heart. "How did you sleep last night, my sweetheart?" Blair murmured.

"I didn't wake up once," I said with a grin.

"Good," he said. "Stick with me; I'll have you sleeping well every night."

I giggled. Blair considered my sleeping well his accomplishment.

A second blurb of music from the alarm and Blair jumped out of bed. I stretched and hopped up, quickly making the king-sized bed. Downstairs I started the coffee and assembled Blair's lunch. *Ah,* I thought, *today's Friday.* Our favorite weekday, for Thursday was a long day, but Friday was short. I loaded the dishwasher with dishes from the busy night before.

After a shower and a shave, Blair came downstairs and poured half-and-half into his coffee. "I nailed it this time," he declared, "just the right sweetness and cream." Blair sipped his coffee, joining me in looking out over the back yard, now surrounded in darkness. We opened our Bibles and got our pens ready.

I had been puzzling over heaven lately. Not because I didn't believe it was real, nor that I didn't believe I was going there, but because I had married for the second time. Bill, I knew was in heaven. Wisha was also in heaven. But what about Blair and me? Jesus said there was no marriage in heaven, yet how would that work? How would we see each other? These different people who had loved *both* mates. I smiled to myself, knowing God's plan was perfect. It was only I who had questions.

"Mmm," I said, letting go of my thoughts while taking my first sip. "I'm not sure what heaven is like," I said, "but it's hard to believe it is better than this cup of coffee with you."

"Oh, heaven will be better for sure," Blair put in.

"You're sure?"

Blair replied with a wise analogy. "You know how you stub your toe and all you can think about is how much it hurts?"

"Yes."

"Well," he continued, "when we get to heaven, all we will see will be Jesus Christ. Just as a hurt toe becomes our main event, *He* will be our main event, and we won't be able to think about anything else. It will be infinite joy."

We continued our morning routine, reading the gospels, praying for the needs of our family and world. Then breakfast, and time for Blair to leave for work. As he walked to the car, he kissed me good-bye.

Lunchtime, Blair called me as usual. "Guess what!" he said excitedly, "Jonathan and Jane have job interviews." Jonathan had gone to Phoenix for flight training, where he had moved in with his Aunt Jane. Meanwhile, Jane had been laid off from her job. For several months now, we'd been praying for both to find employment.

"Let's have a celebration dinner," I suggested.

"Great idea," he agreed.

After work, I checked in with Blair about his workout. "What did Chris make you do today?"

"Oh, we worked on my abs," Blair answered. "I want to have a flat stomach for my sweetheart, you know."

We watched O'Reilly and had our first glass of wine, then started dinner with red pepper soup, working our way to scallops and pasta with pesto.

"I'd rate this a nine," Blair said, holding up his fork.

"Not bad for ten minutes in the kitchen," I laughed.

With full bellies, we settled to watch the unnerving movie, *Eyes Wide Shut*, with Tom Cruise and Nicole Kidman playing a husband and wife. Interestingly, it would be Stanley Kubrick's final movie and also the last movie starring the conflict-ridden couple, their real-life marriage crumbling.

Cruise's character suspected another man of coming on to Kidman's character, and he told her so. She was insulted and angry, not because of the insinuation about the man wanting sex with her, but because of the point he made about her beauty. She didn't want to be called beautiful.

What was wrong with beautiful? We wondered. Didn't Kidman's character carefully choose her dress? Hadn't she also taken the time to attractively apply makeup? I, myself, always looked carefully in the mirror before leaving the house. "So why do you think she felt so insulted?" I asked.

"I don't know," said Blair. "Tell me."

"Women have been taught by society to be insulted when a man first compliments us on our beauty and not our intelligence," I explained. We were suspicious of the power of sex and beauty. At the same time, we paradoxically used them to our benefit. I thought guiltily how, in my first marriage, I had paraded in sexy clothes whenever my husband was upset with me. I'd used sex to get my way.

I had to admit feeling conflicted. Someone might graciously compliment my figure or face and I'd enjoy that, yet at the same time, I'd think, *But do you like what I say? Am I as smart as I am pretty?*

"Women can get pretty confused," I said.

"No wonder they give such confusing signals," Blair concluded.

I promised Blair that I would work on saying what I meant rather than giving subtle hints. I would do my best to deal with problems head-on, rather than use sex to control the other. And, as I had thus far in our relationship, I would accept a compliment of Blair's for what it was: a compliment.

We went upstairs and readied ourselves for bed. I slipped into a silky camisole set and spun around in front of him. "Anyway," I said. "I can still dress up ... just like Nicole."

Blair gave me an enveloping hug and said in his imitable style, "You are *such* a sexy woman!" There was a twinkle in his eye. "I'm not very sleepy. What do you think about that?"

How rich, the rhythms of married love and life!

Chapter 22

Changes

11:30 p.m., January 29, 2010

Blair sat up slowly, his eyes rolling back in his head. I gasped. His expression was blank, confused. A sheen of perspiration covered his pasty brow. "Blair, what's wrong?"

I ran to the bathroom for a cold washcloth and came back to wipe his face. He collected himself, smiled, and turned to me. "Did I frighten you, my sweetheart?"

"Yes. But that's okay. How do you feel now?" I asked anxiously.

The blank look gave way to his normal expression. "Just a bit faint," he said.

"I think you're supposed to put your head between your knees," I suggested.

He willingly tried to bend his neck. Somehow, he slid off the tall bed. Naked, he lay resting his back and head against the bed. "I—I feel like I'm going to throw up," he said.

I dashed away, returning with a bucket. He trembled as he vomited, then apologized for missing the container. Blair, always the gentleman.

"My head kind of hurts," he said. I knelt on the floor beside him and took his pulse. A few moments passed. "I think you should call an ambulance," said Blair.

Other times I might have suggested waiting to see if he felt better. This time, I didn't question, but ran to the phone—it seemed so far away, on the other side of the room. "Someone will be there soon," said the 911 operator. "Turn on the outside lights and open the door."

I threw on a knit shirt and jeans, then dashed downstairs to follow the operator's instructions. *Blair!* I thought. I scrambled back up the stairs. "Let's get you dressed!"

"No," he moaned.

I'd never seen my fastidious husband in such distress. And I'd never moved so fast, letting the firefighters in the instant they arrived.

"What is your name?" one asked Blair.

He told them, leaning against the bed, eyes partly closed.

They asked him what my name was, what day it was, who was the president of the United States. He answered each question correctly, his tongue thick and awkward in his mouth. They worked on his left side, checking his vitals, preparing an IV. One worker got a bath towel to give Blair some covering—and dignity. I quickly knelt by Blair's right side, putting my mouth to his ear. "I love you, Blair." He was strangely quiet, giving no sign of acknowledgement, his head leaning against the bed.

"Oh Lord, intervene," I prayed. "Help Blair and those helping him." I reached for the comfort that had meant so much, just four years earlier. "The Lord is my Shepherd, I shall not want," I recited.

Soon after that, two paramedics came, more skilled than the first. They asked me to move so they could work on Blair. As I turned and stood, I heard a strange snoring heave, moving up through my husband's lungs, terrifying and strange. What did it mean?

I scrambled out of the way quickly and dashed to get my shoes on. He seemed to me to be worsening very quickly. I could hear them discussing what they were doing.

"We got his blood pressure back up," one said. Very quickly, they put a stretcher underneath him and carried the now-unconscious figure downstairs to the ambulance.

I tried to take it all in. "You're not to ride in the ambulance," one technician instructed. "But don't follow us too closely; we'll be moving at top speed."

Oh yes, I thought. *Hurry – please hurry!* I closed up the house and sprinted to my car.

Nick, the neighbor, stepped up to the curb. "What's wrong?"

"I don't know," I said. "A stroke or something."

Nick gave me a quick hug. "Is there anything I can do?"

I shook my head and swallowed.

"Just pray. Pray hard."

He offered to drive me, but I didn't want to waste time. I didn't want to be with anyone just then. Though it was against the law to use the cell phone, I promptly called Erika and Jonathan. I drove down the street taking the long way, distracted. *I probably should have let Nick drive me,* I thought.

At the emergency room, Blair looked gray, weak. Medical personnel had inserted a breathing tube down his throat in the ambulance. They had already given him a brain scan since there was a neurosurgeon on duty. "He's had some bleeding on the brain," said a nurse. "We need to perform a procedure to release some pressure. You'll need to sign some papers."

My mind was screaming, *No, no, no!* The neurosurgeon came to discuss the treatment. It was Dr. Shanno, the neurosurgeon who had done Bill's brain angioplasty. A terrible, despairing wave of memory washed over me. This was the same doctor, with similar dreadful news. Brain damage? Death?

Oh, could I just put everything on "pause" and reverse the situation? I didn't want to be here. *Please!*

I waited in a quiet room. Erika and Connie came, throwing their arms around me. Soon, Pastor Brian Martin joined our small circle.

Dr. Shanno emerged. My heart pounded. "They have finished with the procedure," he announced. "We're sending Blair up to ICU to observe him for the night. We'll possibly do another procedure in the morning." I tried to still myself, find some pocket of hope.

"I should tell you," Dr. Shanno added, "He hasn't responded since we took the pressure off. I don't like it. He is unconscious and unmedicated." My heart sank to the depths, and I floundered.

Somehow I found the courage to say, "You may not remember me, but you did the angioplasty on my late husband's brain a few years ago."

His eyes widened. "Oh. I *do* remember. I'm so sorry." It was a look of sadness, tragedy. There was no hope in that look.

My heart broke. My mind was like a rabid animal, clawing for a hold on reality. Why? We'd had only seventeen months of marriage! I wanted more!

Elevators were shut down for the night, and ER nurse Janet accompanied us to the ICU. "This might look bad," she said, looking at me with eyes full of caring, "but don't give up. I've seen many patients with bleeds on the brain who eventually show radical improvement."

Hold onto hope, I told myself. Then I heard the quiet voice of my God saying, "I am here, daughter. None of this is a surprise to me. I am with you."

Brian Martin waited with us while they readied Blair in his unit. I began to cry, my heart breaking. This was too uncanny. The same hospital, the same neurosurgeon, the same sense of loss. *Why* was I here again? Yet again, the voice reminded, "My plans for Blair are not your plans. I myself have appointed Blair his days."

Brian prayed a simple prayer. "Heavenly Father, if it would be Your will, would you please heal Blair? In the meantime, please give wisdom for those caring for him. Comfort Shirley, and give her peace. In Jesus' name, Amen."

Saturday, January 30, 2009

Sometime in the early morning, I knelt beside Blair in the hospital bed, where his breathing was done by a machine. I put my head on his dear shoulder, trying to get as close as possible with all the surrounding equipment. Oh, if only I could turn the tide. If only I could make him better! Yet, through this terrible turmoil, I felt peace. "Thank you," I told the nurse who came in and adjusted his IV.

"Oh, I appreciate that," I said to Connie when she brought me a hot cup of coffee and muffin, even though I wasn't hungry. Blair was in God's hands, I knew, and He loved him more than I did. My daughter and friend were with me, but God was there too.

During our courtship and marriage, when people asked how I was, I always answered, "fantastic," "super," "great." God had brought this handsome, intelligent, godly man into my lonely widowhood, a man who was crazy-in-love with me, and I with him. People would chuckle, "God is certainly smiling on you." Now, I thought to myself, *God is weeping with me.*

Scripture ran through my mind: *The Lord is my Rock, my fortress and my deliverer ... the horn of my salvation, my stronghold* (Psa. 18:2). *Never will I leave you; never will I forsake you* (Heb. 13:5).

The hours moved quickly forward, yet I felt I was in a vacuum where time had stopped. Connie and Erika were making phone calls to family. Pastor Paul Jackson and his wife, Nancy, arrived, embracing me, at a loss for words. We prayed for Blair—for God's will. *Oh please, God, let it be Your will that Blair recovers.*

As I lay by Blair's side, I looked up to see my ninety-two-year-old mother wheeled into the room by my sister Joyce. "Shirley," Mom said, "You're strong. You can get through this."

I said tearfully, "I don't *want* to be strong; I want my Blair to get better."

Mom trembled and strained in her wheelchair, as if longing to comfort her child by taking her in her arms. Unable to do that, she stretched out her shaking hand to me, tears in her eyes. It was a moment of utter helplessness, surrender, and love.

Sometime later, Dr. Shanno came into the room. "It appears that Blair's brain is dead," he said gravely. "We don't expect him to recover." Words and images blurred in a surreal collage as he showed me films of the brain scans. Clinging to the brain were blotches of black: blood, the doctor explained. Further tests would be performed to confirm the damage.

Greg, Jonathan, and Jane arrived, and after tearful hugs, viewed the films and heard the facts. Pastor Paul touched my arm. "Maybe you and the boys should have some time alone with Blair to say good-bye."

I could hear the quiet rhythm of the breathing machine. My dear, sweet, kind husband was dying. Greg and Jonathan's last surviving parent. My best friend, my lover, my "beloved Boaz." I wanted to run screaming down the hallways.

My sister, Eileen, began singing softly:

"When peace, like a river, attendeth my way,
When sorrows like sea billows blow.
Whatever my lot Thou hast taught me to say
It is well; it is well, with my soul."

My voice shaking, I began to sing with her. Through the sobs and tears, I remembered, Blair's soul was fine and mine would be too. With choked voices we continued our duet.

Amazing grace, how sweet the sound
That saved a wretch like me
I once was lost but now am found
Was blind but now I see.

It was Blair's favorite hymn.

I kept reaching for Blair's hand, hoping he would grasp mine like he usually did. His hand was stiff and unresponsive.

Jane kissed her brother. Then Greg and Jonathan each knelt and kissed his face. And then I bent to him with a kiss, whispering that I loved him.

A jarring transition followed, as nurses ushered us to another room. "You need to decide together about donating Blair's organs," a facilitator informed us. How could we be addressing this so clinically? I would never again see Blair on the earth.

We bravely grappled with the questions. Greg, Jonathan, Jane, Erika, Trent, and I. We decided to donate his kidneys and liver to give others a new chance at life.

They needed to find just the right recipients for his organs and that would take a few hours, so we left to get dinner. Food seemed pointless. The restaurant was crowded, with servers smiling and singing "Happy Birthday" to a red-haired, twenty-something woman who sat behind her cupcake and burning candle, surrounded by laughing, singing family and friends.

How could anyone celebrate on this day? And then with a dull ache in my stomach, I remembered the horrible irony. This *was* Jonathan's thirty-second birthday.

I managed a few bites of chicken before arriving back in Blair's room. I kissed his brow, clasped his hand, begged God to heal him. And then, I surrendered his life to the Giver of Life and asked Him to have His way.

Sunday, January 31, 2010

For the next eight hours, I stayed in Blair's room.

"What are we waiting for?" I asked the nurse, Linda.

"An exact match to receive his organs," she explained. "We never know how long it will take." She turned and adjusted Blair's head on the pillow tenderly, though he couldn't feel a thing. "There," she told him. "That's better."

She turned to me. "You must be exhausted. Can I set up a cot for you?"

I nodded numbly.

"You poor thing," she said, wrapping her arms around me.

"Thanks," I mumbled. Just another embrace from an angel, at exactly the right moment.

I lay down, but couldn't rest. I stood up, got some tea, came back to the room. A verse shimmered in my mind. I had a sudden image of myself as a young girl in my best blue Sunday dress, standing before a classroom reciting scripture. I had memorized it so painstakingly. What a comfort it was to me now!

> *One thing have I desired of the LORD,*
> *that will I seek after;*
> *that I may dwell in the house of the LORD all the days of my life,*
> *To behold the beauty of the LORD,*
> *and to enquire in His temple.*
>
> —Psa. 27:4 KJV

It was all Blair ever wanted. Was he already beholding the beauty of the Lord? Perhaps he was still in deep sleep, waiting for his entry. I took a deep breath.

For in the time of trouble he shall hide me in his pavilion:
in the secret of his tabernacle shall he hide me;
he shall set me up upon a rock. (vs. 5)

A clear voice sang in my mind, a passage set to music:

Fear not, for I am with you
Do not be afraid.

"How are you doing?" Eileen asked on the phone.

"I don't know how," I said, "but I feel peace. Pure, unadulterated peace."

When morning came, Jonathan took me to the house. The bedroom had been straightened up from the mess of emergency equipment, towels, and vomit. I changed out of my jeans and sweater, worn for nearly thirty hours, rumpled and stained with tears.

Back at the hospital, the waiting game continued.

"Tell me a little about you and Blair," said Linda, taking a seat beside me.

I told her how we met, what we did together. "You did so much," she said, "in such a short time!" Truly we had squeezed a lifetime of adventures into just under two years.

Greg, Jonathan, Jane, Eileen, Todd, Erika, and Trent joined me at the bedside. We sang, we prayed. We kissed Blair good-bye. We walked alongside as they finally wheeled the bed away. I kissed him for the last time in his living body. *Good-bye my dearest, so loving, the kindest man in all the earth. You were the best and I am grateful.*

Chapter 23

Without Blair

January 31, 2010

"WHY DID YOU give Blair to me if you were going to snatch him away so quickly?" I raged at God. The words came to mind again which had comforted me after losing Bill. *My frame was not hidden from you when I was made in the secret place, when I was woven together in the depths of the earth. Your eyes saw my unformed body; all the days ordained for me were written in your book before one of them came to be* (Psa. 139:15-16).

There was a gaping hole in my heart. I couldn't stop crying. I didn't know if I could survive. Yet I realized in my raging that I didn't have to understand. I didn't have to be happy about this outcome. I didn't know the torrent of prayers that were being poured out by so many.

Todd squeezed my hand as we drove home from the hospital with Erika and Trent, the last time we would see Blair's living body on earth. "It was just getting good," he whispered.

The Tribe met us at the house where Erika and Trent seated them on the staircase, carefully explaining that Grandpa Blair had died. Emily and Annabel, ages four and five, were too little to understand, but Andrew cried, and Caleb became quiet and serious.

That evening, I lay my head where Blair had placed his just seventy-two hours ago. In all that time, I'd only slept a couple of hours. Now I dozed, forgetting all.

Monday, February 1, 2010

I woke to the nightmare. *My beloved Blair is gone. I am broken.* I then got up to face the day, still crying, sending the announcement of his death over email. Stepping on the scale, I'd lost five pounds. I was sure they were five pounds of tears.

As family and friends near and far responded, so many asked, "What happened? He took such good care of himself!"

We all felt the shock. There was a blessing in having so much to do, preparing for Blair's funeral. *Why did this feel so terribly familiar?* I asked myself, but knew the answer.

Greg wrote the obituary (just as Todd had done four years earlier), made a list, and gave assignments to all. His eyes were rimmed with dark circles from a sleepless night.

Collecting Blair's clothing for burial, I knelt down by his tennis shoes, the socks tucked within and a pair of jeans carelessly flung alongside. With a lump in my throat, I remembered his love-struck hurry in getting to bed that last evening.

Soon, I was sitting at the funeral home office, staring at the same dark walls and scenic mountain photos that I'd stared at four years earlier, almost to the day. I knew where the showroom was for the caskets. I knew the questions that would be asked. There I was. Mourning. Broken. A widow. I *hated* the word "widow." It sounded like a disease.

The funeral director, Denton, was an acquaintance from my high school graduating class. I hadn't seen him since Bill's funeral. Now, the face of someone I knew was comforting. "Shirley, I am so sorry," he said, offering a hug.

Flowers and cards kept arriving at the house. Angels of mercy phoned, offering help. Dorothy, a family friend, brought sandwich makings for lunch and a delicious creamed turkey crepe casserole. Her banana cake finished the meal with a touch of sweetness.

How can I be enjoying this? I wondered with a sudden pang.

I reminded myself that Blair was in perfect bliss. It was his family, friends, students, colleagues, and neighbors who were bereft.

Tuesday, February 2, 2010

A dear friend shared a song from years ago:

> When I think I'm going under
> Part the waters, Lord....[10]

The words meant so much. Truly, through this whole ordeal, He was there, parting the waters, holding out his hand, weeping with me, sad with me, just *there*. I had no proof, nothing except the peace that passes all understanding.

Erika and four-year-old Emily stopped by to visit Greg and me. Emily piped up, "Where's Grandpa Blair?"

Erika answered in a soft voice. "Grandpa Blair went to heaven." Emily looked at us in puzzlement, unable to piece together what she had been told two days ago. It simply made no sense that we would be gathered together when a key person was missing.

Erika and Emily talked as they drove home in the van together. "Dying means you don't live here anymore," said Erika. "Everybody dies sometime. And if Jesus is in your heart," she explained, "you'll be with him in heaven after you die."

"I want to ask Jesus in my heart!" said Emily. Erika reached over, squeezed her hand, and they prayed.

The angels were rejoicing for "Emilee," using the name Blair had given her. He was rejoicing too.

Blair's sister Jane didn't like the idea of my sleeping all alone in that big bed at night. "A person gets used to another warm body," she said, and tucked in beside me with her novel and cup of tea on the nightstand.

She talked to me. Told me stories about Blair. "We were ushers at The Forum together. It was such fun to be with my big brother." She told me her version of the trip to South Africa for his wedding to Wisha.

In the morning we blinked at each other sleepily. "How was my snoring? Not too bad I hope?" she asked.

"Well, you definitely snored," I laughed, "but it was good to have you here."

I had memorized every word of her stories, desperate for more of the husband I'd had for such a short time.

Sometimes I would ask myself, *Was I really married to him? Was it really that good?* And I would answer, *Yes. Oh, yes.*

Wednesday, February 3, 2010

I can't possibly wear the same black suit I wore for Bill's service, I told myself. It seemed strange and wrong. So Erika joined me on a shopping trip, where, before long, I was stopped by a sales person asking the conventional, "How are you?"

"I'm not good," I responded.

"Oh," said the sales person, taken aback.

There was an awkward silence, and then I explained, "I'm looking for a dress to wear at my late husband's memorial service." I failed to keep the quiver from my voice.

"I understand," she answered, giving me a sad smile. She helped me find a black suit with a cream-colored blouse, classy and beautiful, to wear in honor of my classy husband. I could always wear it again, I thought. But to this day it hangs in my closet, the shawl collar holding tightly to sad memories.

After shopping, we met Pastor Paul at our home, together with the rest of the family. He was collecting stories about Blair.

Pastor Paul asked each of us what we would like shared at the service. I said, "I want people to know what a good husband he was, both to me and to his first wife." I continued, "More than anything, I want people to know about Blair's faith in Jesus. He prayed every day for his students, family, country."

Jonathan relayed how during his high school years he and his dad had a talk about how it would be in school, for Jonathan would be in his classroom.

"When in school, Jonathan, you will call me Mr. Graybill, and I will call you Jonathan," Blair told him.

Greg told how after school, Blair would toss the football around with the boys and then see to it Jonathan did his homework. He was intentional in teaching them how to do things in an orderly fashion. There was a stack of wood to split and stack in their back yard. Blair would demonstrate how it was done. Cut the wood like so, then stack it like this. He then told them he'd inspect the stack later on, expecting the job to be done right. He did it in a gracious, kind, and methodical way.

Greg wanted it to be known that his father was a sinner, saved by grace, and only belief in the Son of God, the person of Jesus Christ, was what made him good.

Both boys told how Blair loved football. He loved it when he played it as a boy in high school and one year of college. But he also loved to coach it. And he was good at it. But when his own boys began to get older, he realized, with Wisha's urging too, that he needed to be home with his boys in their crucial teen years.

The sons watched their dad treat their mother with love and grace—through to the end while she struggled with cancer. He was a great example of how to be a husband. He modeled for his boys what he would expect from his sons. And as they became men, he treated them as men, walking alongside them.

There was an evening visitation at the funeral home for friends and family to pay their respects to the immediate family and if they desired, to see Blair one last time. Blair's coffin was in an alcove and in the front of the chapel, we had photos from various seasons of Blair's life. It was comforting to see the photos and Blair so alive. What a contrast to his still body in the alcove.

As I gazed at Blair's body, so still in the coffin, I thought back at seeing my own dear father, looking at him in death. I touched my father's hand and it was stiff and cold, statue-like. I recoiled. That was not my dad! It gave me fear to ever touch another loved one in death. When Bill was there, in his coffin, I was afraid to touch for I didn't want that stiffness memory.

Jonathan and I looked at Blair together. I said, "I want to touch him, but I'm afraid." I went on to tell him my experience with my dad. "Maybe I'll ask Denton what it would be like to touch him."

So I did and Denton said, "He will feel cool, not stiff."

I bravely reached out and touched Blair's hand. It was an important part of this ritual. "He's right. It just feels cool," I whispered. Jonathan touched his father too. We each said our good-byes to the still form that really did not seem like Blair.

Greg and Jonathan later stood in front of the closed casket with their hands on the top as Greg prayed.

Thursday, February 4, 2010

Caytie arrived from Pittsburgh on Wednesday evening and our family was complete. Meanwhile, many continued to arrive from out of town. These included cousins from Florida, Blair's brother and his wife from San Diego, in-laws from Pennsylvania, and members of my family from Arizona and California.

As I waited for Connie and Eileen to arrive for our drive together to the Walla Walla graveside service, I began to feel very angry. I wanted to throw something. I stormed around the house, packing my things, asking God out loud. "Why have You done this, Lord? I don't like this one bit. I want out!" I was shocked at my angry feelings. I railed at God at the dual losses each family member had suffered. I had lost two husbands. Greg and Jonathan had lost two parents. My children had lost two fathers, my grandchildren had lost two grandpas. Why? Once again my life was abruptly changed.

Yet, in that anger and railing, I felt peace. There was no joy, only great sorrow, yet peace too. This wasn't something I worked up from within myself, but the Holy Spirit worked in me. Comforting me. Even though I didn't know it, healing my broken heart too.

My sister-in-law Lexie's friend Ceil, shared a meal in her home Thursday evening. She prepared a chicken enchilada casserole with stuffed ortegas, along with wines, condiments, and a salad. She served the dinner smorgasbord-style to nearly thirty guests.

Friday, February 5, 2010

The graveside could have been a movie set. I wished it were, and not the real thing. It was raining. I thought, *I'm glad it's raining. The skies are weeping along with my heart.*

Dick and Greg stood in front of the casket, quiet and still. As I looked at them, I wondered, *Greg is so strong. How can he do this?* I sat opposite them with close family members nearby. Greg read, *Brothers and sisters, we do not want you to be uninformed about those who sleep in death, so that you do not grieve like the rest of mankind, who have no hope* (1 Thess. 4:13).

I wanted to say good-bye to Blair privately. Yet people seemed to stay around and not want to leave me alone. There were snatches of conversation, old friends catching up on their latest news, just outside the canopy over the grave.

"Hi Joe, it's good to see you." Laughter. Hugs exchanged. "How've you been?" "Did your son get that job he was looking for?"

I know they didn't do this on purpose, but I hated it. At last, someone asked them to move some place else.

I watched my daughter and her family as they walked to their van. Little Emily was the last tripping along over the gravel, with her tiny legs in white tights and black patent leather shoes. She held tightly to her mother's hand, aware something very serious was happening, but she wasn't sure what.

A dinner provided by friends from Walla Walla was served to us at the College Place Presbyterian church. I was able to meet and see close friends from Walla Walla there. The boys were able to meet their parents' old friends—and theirs too. I spoke with Dale Newby, who was the friend who asked Blair to his first Walk to Emmaus where Blair accepted Christ as his Lord and Savior. After retiring as principal of the local school, Dale became a financial planner and we had met with him just the previous summer to discuss options for Blair's upcoming retirement. Dale asked me. "Are you the beneficiary of Blair's retirement?" He was concerned that I'd be taken care of.

"Yes. Blair took care of all of that."

"That's good. That was the right thing to do," he said.

Others greeted me and introduced themselves. I recognized names Blair had talked about, friends and colleagues in Walla Walla. Jeff and Jane Krietzberg told me to come and stay with them anytime.

The skies began to clear. This was all right now. Weeping had been done for a time. Todd needed good weather to return to Vancouver in his airplane and it would mean better driving conditions for all.

When we arrived back home, dear friends from Portland Christian School served a delicious pasta dinner. It felt good to be cared for by so many.

During this time, I was flooded with scripture passages from the Psalms. *My flesh and my heart may fail, but God is the strength of my heart and my portion forever* (Ps. 73:26). *Call on me in the day of trouble; I will deliver you and you will honor me.* (Ps. 50:15). *Be still, and know that I am God* (Ps. 46:10 NKJ).

I reminded myself of WHO God is: *For the word of the LORD is right and true; he is faithful in all he does* (Ps. 33:4). *To you, LORD, I call; you are my Rock* (Ps. 28:1). *All the ways of the Lord are loving and faithful* (Ps. 25:10). And then Psalm 23, the passage I memorized at age four, a scripture my mom had each of us children memorize at that age. *The LORD is my shepherd ... and I will dwell in the house of the LORD forever."*

My beloved Blair was dwelling there now.

Chapter 24

Good-bye, Blair Graybill

Memorial Weekend, February 6-7, 2010

The Dance

This is the story of Shirley. One day, she met Bill when both were very young. They began to dance. It was sometimes awkward. No matter how they tried, they kept stepping on each other's toes. Yet, they knew if they looked to the One who created the dance, He would help them, and He did. As the years passed, their dance flowed, smooth and beautiful. And then, Bill was gone.

Shirley thought she would never dance again. A part of her longed to, but it had taken so much work for her and Bill to get it right, she wasn't sure she had the energy.

Then one day, Shirley met Blair and they began to dance. Their dance was a little faster, but smooth from the start. Both could hardly believe how easy it was, with never an awkward moment. Then, just as quickly as Blair showed up, he was gone. If Shirley had known that her heart would hurt so much, she might not have let Blair have her dance card. But she would have missed the dance of a lifetime.

—Heidi Timm

Second Chances

THE DAY OF the memorial service dawned with clear blue skies, in contrast to the graveside service. We arrived at the church, where cars were already thick in the parking lot. People flocked around us, telling how sorry they were. The connections were astounding. Mike Robbins, Blair's college roommate, was there. He was the pilot who had flown Todd's chase plane on its maiden voyage of the *Hot to Go*.

The church was brightly decorated with mementoes, photos, and a red, white, and blue banner featuring both the American and Confederate flags, hand-drawn by one of Blair's students. There were heaps of letters from students, offering appreciation and love and from fellow teachers, expressing admiration for Blair's wisdom, knowledge, and insight.

Pastor Paul rescued our small family group from the onslaught of people and took us to his study to wait for the service. Muttering through the hallway, I said, "I am not going through this again. Twice is enough!"

Greg in his calm way turned to me. "Whatever you want to do," he said simply.

Such a Blair-like response to my crazy grieving statement. I collected myself and stood up straighter, determined not to feel sorry for myself. As we entered the sanctuary, Todd escorted me on his arm. It was strangely like that beautiful day seventeen months earlier.

The service began with talented violinist Jed Bartowski, in a flawless performance of "Ashokan Farewell," the haunting theme song from the Civil War television series by Ken Burns.

My favorite Psalm was read. *The LORD is my light and my salvation—whom shall I fear? The LORD is the stronghold of my life—of whom shall I be afraid? For in the day of trouble, he will keep me safe in his dwelling; he will hide me in the shelter of his sacred tent and set me high upon a rock. I remain confident of this: I will see the goodness of the LORD in the land of the living. Wait for the LORD; be strong and take heart and wait for the LORD.* (Ps. 27:1, 5, 13-14)

Pastor Paul began to read the obituary Greg had written.

"Henry Blair Graybill II was born on November 12, 1944 to Harry and Martha Jane O'Connell Graybill in Clifton Forge, Virginia."

I tried hard not to cry while Paul continued. I felt the strength of my family next to me, Todd on one side, Erika and Trent on my other side, Greg and Caytie, Jonathan and his girlfriend, Mar, in the same row, next to us.

> "Surviving are his wife, Shirley, sons, Gregory (Cathryn) and Jonathan Graybill; daughter, Erika (Trent) Sagert and their four children, Andrew, Caleb, Annabel, and Emily; son, Todd Rudberg and his two daughters, Rebekah and Sarah, brothers John (Andrienne) and Oscar (April) Graybill; and sister, Jane Graybill."

Greg hadn't distinguished in the obituary between children and stepchildren. I was touched and pleased.

We sang as a congregation:

When we've been there ten thousand years
Bright shining as the sun
We've no less days to sing God's praise
Than when we first begun.[11]

Oh what great hope was in that last verse! I thought back to when we'd sung "Amazing Grace" at our wedding, with tears of joy running down Blair's face. Was he weeping with joy this time, too? Perhaps he was so full of joy and contentment in heaven, he couldn't feel how stricken we were without him.

Greg read: *"Do not let your hearts be troubled. You believe in God; believe also in me. My Father's house has many rooms; if that were not so, would I have told you that I am going there to prepare a place for you? And if I go and prepare a place for you, I will come back and take you to be with me that you also may be where I am. You know the way to the place where I am going"* (John 14:1-4). *"All this I have spoken while still with you. But the Advocate, the Holy Spirit, whom the Father will send in my name, will teach you all things and will remind you of everything I have said to you. Peace I leave with you; my peace I give you. I do not give to you as the world gives. Do not let your hearts be troubled and do not be afraid"* (John 14: 25-27). Greg explained that Blair put his trust in his Savior, Jesus Christ, and he was alive in heaven. It wasn't because Blair was such a good man, but because he trusted Christ. He encouraged those who did not believe and trust in Christ to repent of their sins and have the new life God promises to give through His son, Jesus Christ.

Blair's sister, Jane, said to me later, "Greg's message was so clear. I understand the gospel better than I ever have before."

Paul gave the eulogy and message, "A Life Well Lived." He told Greg's story of how Blair would regularly call him and Caytie, until one day the calls seemed to drop off. Blair left a voicemail saying, "I've met someone and am dating her. Goodbye." We all laughed at that.

Paul directed the next part to me in the front row. "I really don't have the words, Shirley, to truly capture your love for Blair and his love for you. It was one of those 'you-have-to-see-it-to-believe-it' kind of things." He continued, "I am so grateful to God for giving you the time He did. God will continue to be faithful to you in this life and in the life to come." He added, "Blair loved you, Shirley. Blair also loved Jesus Christ."

Paul told my story of our last devotion together, when Blair declared that heaven would be better than life here on earth. God had given him a slice of heaven on earth with our marriage. Yet heaven itself was even greater.

"… much greater than we can ever imagine," Paul continued, "because of Who is in heaven. The God who loves us. His Son who embraces us and receives us. So heaven is greater than we could ever imagine. God offers a gift to all of us in Christ—yours for the asking." He closed with the question, "Will you ask?"

My farewell letter was read:

My dearest Blair—my beloved Boaz,

I feel so privileged to have experienced the deep love and oneness we shared. I simply couldn't get enough of you—and you of me. We had so many things that we planned to do. Yet, what we did, in our short married life, some people don't do in a lifetime! Thank you, my love. For your unconditional love. For your kindness. For your encouragement. For your family who is now *my* family. For your loving me and my children and grandchildren as if they were your own. For your love of the Savior. I'm so glad you made that decision to follow Christ thirty-five years ago and that we will be reunited again in heaven. And when I get there, my life here on Earth will be a blink compared to the eternity we will experience with our Lord Jesus Christ and others who follow Him.

I will continue to love your boys as though they were mine by birth. I already do! I will be Grammie to your grandchildren to come, as you were Grandpa to mine. I will continue to be grateful for you and our bond that only death separates for a time.

All my love,
Shirley

We watched a video collage of Blair's life, photos of childhood, young adulthood (what a hunk of a man!), marriage and children, his later life, and then our life together.

Trent spoke of how Blair included our family in his family. How he taught Trent's sons to love football. How he admired that we prayed together each day. One colleague spoke of his knowledge and love of history. Another stood and told of his integrity and the love he had for his first wife and how he suffered because *she* suffered. And then he told how after a period of time he was ready to meet someone, and soon after how smitten he was with me.

We were dismissed to a piano rendition of "The Battle Hymn of the Republic," the crucial Civil War song. The unsung chorus rang in my head, as if to rally me to life. *Glory, glory, hallelujah! Our God is marching on!*

The reception line was long. So many wanted to see me and talk. It began to seem as if *they* were the ones needing comfort, and

I was the one to give it. Weary, I pulled up a chair as I continued to converse with people. When we finally returned home, family members said their goodbyes and I prepared for one last special celebration for Blair.

Sunday, February 7, 2010

Sitting at church, filling a full row with my family next to me, I couldn't help but reflect on the last worship service I attended. How sweet was Blair's company! He'd been by my right side, as always, where he could whisper to me, since I was deaf in my left ear.

After church, we went home to prepare our "Super Bowl Wake." Friends at Brush Prairie Baptist provided sandwich makings and desserts, as well as breakfast earlier for those staying at the house. How heartbreakingly different this was than the Super Bowl Party Blair and I had imagined! Yet how blessed I was with my generous Christian community!

Jonathan, Mar, Kevin, and Digger Graybill, Greg, and my grandsons Andrew and Caleb settled in to enjoy the game between the Indianapolis Colts and the New Orleans Saints. The stadium crowd roared and murmured from the television set. I could hear Andrew exclaiming "Yes!" with every New Orleans touchdown, while Colts fans moaned in disgust. Friends and family wandered in and out of the kitchen, helping themselves to the mountains of food and drink. However, there was an empty seat in the living room: Blair's favorite leather chair.

Todd showed up with a load of chicken to make hot wings. "Erika, would you help me with this?" he asked his little sister.

Boxes of photos and letters spilled across the dining table. Blair's family members, Linda and Tom, John and Andy were looking at them with interest. Others thumbed through old photos and letters. "Oh look at this. Is that Aunt Sue?" John asked his cousin, Linda.

"Isn't she cute?" Linda picked up another photo. "And that's Grandfather Graybill, holding Blair."

Some played dominoes. Andy Graybill teamed with Eileen, while my sister-in-law, Lexie and April Graybill made a team. Lexie explained the strategy. Later, since the sun was out, some of us took a walk in the waning winter sun. The forest nearby was full of evergreens waving in a breeze nearly warm on our faces.

The game was over. New Orleans won. Todd asked if Jonathan wanted to go on a flight in his airplane. "Sure!" he agreed, jumping up. The day was perfect with clear blue skies, little wind. Andy and John and Mar came along as well, to have a look at the sporty red, white, and blue airplane Todd had built with his dad. It all seemed so long ago now.

Later, I watched our wedding DVD upstairs in my bedroom. Erika, Caytie, Andy, and Connie offered me their company as women.

But Eileen touched my arm. "Are you sure you want to do this?" Eileen asked with doubt in her face.

"I am."

The camera panned, showing guests walking into the church and then, there was Blair, wonderful, smiling, and handsome in his tux. Whole and healthy.

That's all it took. I melted in tears of anguish. My dear girlfriends—and they were girlfriends even though related to me, surrounded me on the bed. One had her arms around me and all wanted to hold me to take the terrible hurt away. Joining hands, they began to pray audibly, each asking for peace, healing comfort, and God's holy presence. I remember the peace that came over me. Christ Jesus, my comforter was there. It was a holy moment.

While I sat drying my tears, Trent came through the door. "Would you come and talk to Caleb? He's having a hard time. He needs you."

Reluctantly, I left for the toy room and there was Caleb on the bed, sobbing.

"Why are you crying, sweetheart?" I asked.

"Because Grandpa Blair's and my team lost," he sniffed, wiping away the tear stains. These were the first tears he'd shed over Grandpa Blair.

Blair and his grandsons had talked about their favorites. Caleb and his Grandpa Blair had a special bond in rooting together for the Colts. I hugged him and held him close. "It's OK, Caleb. We are all sad. I will be sad for a long time," I continued. "But we have each other. Can we promise each other to give a hug when we're feeling sad?"

Caleb stopped crying. "Okay," he said, reaching out to return my hug.

It was a weekend full of sadness and remembering, of honor and celebration. Only God would be able to fill that terrible, yawning hole that was in our hearts of that wonderful man who was husband, father, stepfather, grandfather, brother, cousin, friend.

Chapter 25

Moving Forward

It seemed cruel to move on, for I wanted to move *back*. My thoughts were jumbled and schizophrenic. When I pushed Blair from my mind, I felt guilty, yet I knew I needed to clear a path forward. With each pair of Blair's socks I dropped into the laundry, with each time I straightened a shirt on its hanger or folded his jeans, I fought conflicting emotions. Tossing Blair's toothbrush, giving away his Sunday baseball cap, I felt I was saying I didn't care anymore.

Greg, Jonathan, and I shared a farewell dinner at Applewood, where Blair and I had our first date. Next morning, Greg was off to Pittsburgh. The weather was spring-like so Jonathan and the grandsons joined me in trimming and cleaning up flower beds. "Where do you want these, boss?" Jonathan asked, carrying a handful of clippings.

I straightened, looking around the yard, which had been Blair's responsibility. Blair knew each plant, its dormant season and when it needed trimming. Now I had to figure everything out on my own.

The days dragged by, including a bleak Valentine's Day. I spent my nights awake, urging the dawn to come. On a Sunday morning after coffee, I threw myself on the stairs, weeping. In the shower, it was as though I were being whipped with the grief. I cried out to

God in my distress, *I don't think I can take it!* There I stood, naked before my God, who knew all about me. I was never hidden from Him. I toweled off, dried my tears, and dressed for church.

Each morning I opened the mailbox, cheered by the sight of a card or note which I placed in a basket. If not for these gestures of kindness, I would have had nothing to look forward to. When my soul felt most wounded, I would choose a note from the basket, savoring the words like a healing balm.

A friend wrote, "I read in Zephaniah about God guiding us by the hand until He eventually guides us to glory. I love the picture I have in my mind of God holding your hand as you walk this rough road." And so I walked forward, but not alone.

I invited friends to join me at the symphony, where I had season tickets. With a companion next to me, the sting of the loss was softened. Yet the one I wanted so badly by my side was not there. "Do you have any gum?" Blair would ask whenever he was getting sleepy and needed a distraction. He'd squeeze my hand, telling me *I love you.* He'd whisper, "I *like* that song!" and smile his affectionate smile. No more.

Attending a choir concert, I was missing Blair terribly when I was arrested by the words of Brahms' Requiem: "Blessed are they that mourn, for they shall have comfort. They that sow in tears shall reap in joy. Who goeth forth and weepeth, and beareth precious seed shall doubtless return with rejoicing and bring his sheaves with him."

FEBRUARY 19, 2010

In my morning room, surrounded by the wicker furniture, I watched spring unfold: leaves budding, tulips poking their greenery up through the soil. Bundled in my robe, reading Scripture, I heard a "thump, thump, thump." I went on reading, but the sound continued. I checked the front of the house and didn't see anything. Again, that persistent sound. I sighed and checked the back. Nothing.

Again, the strange, compelling thump. I got up to check in the garage. As I walked by the powder room window I noticed a large, red breasted robin perched on a small tree just outside.

Next morning, right on cue, I heard the thump again. I watched at the window, where Mr. Robin tapped his beak on the glass and peered in as if he had a message for me.

I reluctantly lowered the shade so he wouldn't see his reflection: I didn't want him to hurt himself. Yet he returned to this window for another two weeks. I knew that robins protect their territory this way during the nesting season, yet it hadn't happened here the previous spring. This cheery, feathered angel sought me out, announcing his presence, letting me know I mattered.

I noted in my journal: "Faith is deliberate confidence in the character of God whose ways you may not understand at this time."—Oswald Chambers.

Later that spring, I attended my nephew's wedding in Arizona. There were family get-togethers, great food, a baseball game, a hike up Camelback Mountain. Jonathan joined us with his comforting presence. Now that Blair was gone, I saw extraordinary similarities between them that I'd never noticed before.

Surrounded by family, things didn't seem so bad. Yet, the visit didn't last forever and I returned home, dragging my suitcase up the stairs. There was no one to remark to about how cold the house was.

Life scenes ambushed me. One afternoon in early June, I was at orchestra rehearsal. Anyone who has ever played a stringed instrument understands the difficulties. There is the pitch. Yes, there is a position for each pitch, but it all depends on where the finger is, how wide it is, and whether you're holding your wrist high enough. Then there is the note. What is the key for this song? Is it a sharp, or flat? Then there is the bowing. Bowing is as important in the violin as playing the correct notes. The bow is drawn across the strings between the fingerboard and bridge, a two inch area. Is it an up-bow, or down-bow? You must follow the music as well as match the other violinists. Does the bow have enough rosin on it to make it bow smoothly? Will you use vibrato?

With all the rigors of playing in an orchestra, I could be removed from my life for a moment, thinking only of the music and my instrument. We were playing James Bond movie themes and struck up with *Live and Let Die*. Blair would have enjoyed this medley, I knew. So often movies had been a touchstone for conversations: "Where were you when this played?" "Did you see the movie?" "Did you like that song?" The tears begin to fall as I remembered. Then we began to play "Nobody Does It Better" and more tears slid down my face, dampening my collar. You, Blair, did it better than anyone!

For Father's Day, our tradition to hike the Tri-Mountain Marathon would not be denied. I suggested broadening the Bill Rudberg Memorial into a "Dad's Memorial Hike." Anyone could take on any stretch of the twenty-five miles and 8,000 feet of elevation in honor of a father, living or dead. Greg and Jonathan joined us, honoring their father that first Father's Day without him.

We also celebrated the birthdays of Erika and Greg, which were one day apart. On Sunday, we sat in church together, then watched the memorial DVD's of both fathers. Then, as with all visits, it came to an end.

A day or so later, I came into the house from the bright sunshine. My eyes were adjusting to the dimness in the cool house when I glanced up—and there in the dining room stood Blair. He was his neat self, in his short sleeved shirt. *You didn't die!* I thought. *Oh, I missed you so much.* But then, reality struck. I blinked and he was gone.

Visitors brought me comfort; my brother and his wife, Lexie, Betsy and her husband, Lyle. Mom was becoming even more frail, and we all visited her. It was good to have someone to share a cup of coffee with in the morning. But they, too, had their own lives and soon I was alone again. My emotions lurched from great sadness to anger. I began to see my life as a story of a long-awaited dessert.

After Bill died, I was like a person no longer allowed sweets. For two years, I went without the richness that a companion brings. And then, the regimen was over. I was told I could have any dessert I wanted. I looked around in anticipation and found *that one*: a luscious piece of mocha chocolate cake with custard filling and chocolate icing. I sat down with a big cup of dark French Roast coffee to chase it down. Our courtship and wedding was my first bite, my taste buds exploding. The second bite, our married life. I set down the plate for a sip of coffee and with a jerk, my cake was taken away. "That's it," said a voice.

Oh I wanted more. *Give me more. More!* I wanted to throw myself down in a tantrum. I railed at God. I hated this terrible sadness.

An old hymn read: "Whate'er my God ordains is right: His holy will abideth; I will be still whate'er He doth; And follow where He guideth. He is my God; though dark my road, He holds me that I shall not fall: Wherefore to Him I leave it all … His hand can turn my griefs away, and patiently I wait His day … And so to Him I leave it all."[12]

I visited Mom every week, and she would hold my hand in her trembling grip. I read Greg's sermons to her as she sat in her chair, a gentle smile on her face. One was titled: "Too Little, Too Late?" It ministered to me as I read to her. Greg explained that John's gospel is known as the spiritual gospel and goes deep. He asked the question: How do you handle sickness and death and unanswered prayers and hostility and impossible odds? We both needed to hear this one. One of the last sermons I read to her was titled "The Resurrection and the Life." How appropriate for this stage of her life. Though Mom lived like she would live forever, she knew her life was winding down. As I read this, she would assent with a "yes," or, "I agree." She understood my pain. She too had been widowed twice.

"Sometimes," she said, "we have to move forward when we don't want to."

One step forward, I decided, was to watch our wedding DVD. I asked my friend, Connie, to join me on the couch in support. With a click of a button, there he was! Whole. Alive. Trembling with emotion as he took his vows. Through my tears, I was strangely comforted.

Another step: I treated myself to a facial. The esthetician was a woman from Ireland. I loved her soothing, smooth lilting accent as she asked about me. I told her my story, and her eyes shone with tears. "Listen," she said. "You will certainly have a man in your life again. Take this time to enjoy your singleness. Go out to dinner by yourself. Decide what you want to eat. Where you want to sit. When you want to leave."

Taking her advice to heart, I bravely planned to celebrate our second wedding anniversary alone, at a lovely, newly-restored Portland Victorian bed and breakfast. I walked myself to an Italian restaurant in the summer heat. Sipping my lemon drop, I savored my favorite pasta—gorgonzola tortellini with red peppers and spinach in a cream sauce.

When dessert came, I sighed at my own little story of the chocolate cake. Here, at least, was chocolate I could enjoy to the last crumb. It wasn't much comfort. I wasn't able to sleep much that night, but I accepted all of this. I was doing the work of grieving.

"Only people who are capable of loving strongly can also suffer great sorrow," Leo Tolstoy said, "but this same necessity of loving serves to counteract their grief and heal them."

I certainly loved strongly. I prayed I would heal.

Then, another step forward. I decided to take each grandchild on a trip. I invited Andrew, age 11, to visit Greg and Caytie in Pennsylvania. Andrew, a wiry, active boy looked up at me excitedly as we took off in the jet at PDX, his light blue eyes bright.

"I can't believe I'm really here!" he said. His nose had a sprinkling of summertime freckles and his light brown hair was mussed up from his baseball cap, now removed. He picked up the library book he was reading, *Spy for George Washington*, in preparation for visiting the Spy Museum later in Washington DC.

We had a great time, exploring covered bridges, visiting Greg's churches, gawking at the city of Pittsburgh, and admiring the green beauty of rural Pennsylvania. One lazy Saturday afternoon, Andrew and I made a homemade apple pie. While it was baking in the oven, Aunt Caytie suggested she and Andrew watch the movie trilogy *Lord of the Rings*. While they experienced the adventures of Aragorn, Sam and Frodo, Uncle Greg and I read our books and the fragrant smells of warm apples and cinnamon made us hungry. By now, the second movie had begun and we enjoyed warm apple pie and lots of whipped cream on top.

Later, Andrew and I rented a car and drove to Charlottesville, Virginia, to visit Monticello and Ash-Lawn Highlands, the homes of Thomas Jefferson and James Monroe. Blair had been a guide at both locations.

While planning our trip, I mentioned to several of my friends about my hesitation in driving by myself on the freeways and toll ways of the East Coast. Many advised me to "Just use a GPS and you'll be fine." I opted to use my Automobile Club Maps and a trip planner. When we picked up our rental car at the Pittsburgh airport, the clerk asked, "Would you like to rent a GPS for only $12 a day?"

"Sure," I said, remembering my friend's advice.

An hour and a half later, after hearing "Madge" tell us she was "recalculating" as we circled the airport for eighty miles, I stopped at a parking lot in frustration. I had a self-talk for a few minutes. "Listen, Shirley. If Mom can drive from Phoenix to Portland *by herself* at age eighty, you can do it!" I said to Andrew, "OK, we are going to first pray, then turn this GPS off and use the maps. You can follow the directions and watch for the exit numbers."

We prayed and at last we were driving through the hilly country of West Virginia. Each turn of the two-lane highway brought a new surprise: a red barn with shining ponies in the pasture, a small town with a general store and gas pumps out front where I wanted to stop and talk to the people with their soft, southern accents. Scenes reminded me of "The Waltons," a favorite TV show from the past.

At last, we reached Charlottesville, Virginia, and our reserved hotel. After a good night's rest, we headed for Monticello. I wanted to run up to every museum staff member and squeal, "Did you know Blair Graybill? Did you work with him? Did you get to experience the friendship of this wonderful man?" I realized I had to let go. I needed to enjoy this trip, here and now.

Next, we drove for three hours to Washington DC venturing into high traffic areas with Andrew as navigator. We took the

Metro for the first time. Andrew paid attention to the stops along the way and informed me when it was time to get off. We climbed to the top of the Washington Monument, exploring all of the free Smithsonian museums, visiting the Spy Museum. My time with Andrew was one of adventure, learning, and a new sense of joy, returning to my heart.

Caleb brought his own words of healing. After church one Sunday, my fourth grandchild handed me a neatly-colored picture of a boy sitting on a high rock with a scripture verse from Matthew 6:34: *Therefore do not worry about tomorrow, for tomorrow will worry about itself. Each day has enough trouble of its own.*

With that, I realized I had been spoiling my joy, worrying over my loss. I stopped worrying. Instead, I began to celebrate all the joy. I had totally, fully enjoyed my nearly perfect husband! And the phrase: "I was dumb with silence because thou didst it" allowed me to know God was in this—and I could rest in that.

Chapter 26

God Is Good

MY MOTHER'S CAREGIVER called me. "She's not doing well," he said. "I think you'd want to be with her now."

"I'll be right over," I said. It took me twenty minutes to drive to the foster home, and when I rushed in the door, it was strangely quiet. The caregiver met me with the news. My mother, Rose Ann Quiring, had died. I stood, bathed in a strange numbness. I could not take in any more sorrow. I would feel this loss later, when I could feel again.

I would never forget the day she died. It was Blair's birthday.

Monday, November 15, 2010

I was driving to the funeral home, this time with Eileen. I clenched my jaw in anger. Once again, I was picking out a casket, selecting clothing. It seemed like a cruel joke.

Yet my mom was freed from her failing body and for that I was happy. In midst of all my emotions, I wanted a husband to place his arms around me, to share my sorrow.

Both Bill and Blair had loved Mom as I did.

Then I realized. Blair and I had never had the chance to experience loss together, just joy and newness. We never felt the beautiful comfort of the other's presence in hard times. Unshared sorrow—now *that* was a sorrow.

JANUARY 23, 2011

It was time for another grandchild trip. Sarah, age 14, wanted sun and water, so we went to Hawaii for four days. Walking through the airport and out into the balmy, humid air, soothed by a light breeze, I was flooded with memories of my honeymoon with Blair.

Everywhere I turned, I was assailed by the sight of couples. An elderly man gently supported his wife's arm as she stepped off the trolley. A young couple, arm in arm, happily chatted as they walked down the beach, their slim, young bodies scantily clad in swimsuits. And a couple in their early sixties, neatly dressed, sat down at a candlelit table. The couple could have been Blair and me—or Bill and me. They reached out across the table, grasping hands. Yet each day I found strength to lift me above the heartbreak. *I will start my day now, dear Lord,* I prayed. *Without my wonderful husband, but with my sweet granddaughter, Sarah, a beautiful young lady and I pray her faith will continue to grow.*

JANUARY 29, 2011

On the one-year anniversary of Blair's death, I had to go somewhere, be with someone who understood. I flew to San Francisco to stay with my brother and his wife, and at the same time, to visit Jonathan to celebrate his birthday. We played dominoes, ate birthday cake and wonderful food Lexie prepared, and I remembered Blair. Sunday morning as we walked through the farmer's market and I was feeling sad, Jonathan came up to me and put his arm around me asking, "You doin' OK, boss?"

"No, I'm not."

That was all the conversation. We both understood we'd have these moments for some time to come. I was grateful when the day, January 31, the anniversary of Blair's death was past. And then, it was time for the Super Bowl once again. Five years ago, I'd been sitting with Pastor Paul while planning Bill's memorial service.

Meanwhile, the Super Bowl played in the other room while Connie watched young Andrew and Caleb.

Two years ago, Blair and I watched the Super Bowl quietly at home. Who had played? I can't remember. But Blair always rooted for the underdog.

One year ago, we held a Super Bowl Wake in honor of Blair. The house was full of people rooting for their team. Blair's team lost.

This year, Andrew and Caleb, ages 10 and 11 both wanted Green Bay to win. Green Bay did. Blair would surely have joined them in rooting for the underdog team.

In the upcoming Super Bowl, I'll be watching the game. I won't be alone, there'll be family there. I'll watch it, not necessarily because I love football so much but because *Blair* loved it. And I loved him.

Dear Blair,

Your bright silver hair seemed to dim when you flashed your smile. Your warm, kind eyes caressed me. Your wonderful, encouraging words. Lifted me up. As quickly as you came into my life, you left. Making me want to aspire to more—a better me!

I woke up this morning with a thought churning in my mind. What would it have been like if I were the one who died and you were left behind? I can see you, working on your stamp albums again. While we were together, I was a happy distraction from this hobby. You would putter around the house and yard. Would your heart break every time you opened the coat closet and saw my red leather jacket? On Sunday, I'm going to Walla Walla where your grave is.

Oh, my love, it tears my heart apart to say goodbye. I love you so very much. I will do my part in telling your grandchildren about Christ, and they will trust Him for salvation and meet you in heaven. My only regret is that we didn't have enough time, but God is sovereign and I must trust Him.

Good-bye for now,
my manly man.
Shirley

One night I had a dream. Wisha came near, gave me a pat on the leg and sat down next to me. "I understand what you've gone through," she said. She had been traveling a long way and lay down on the bench, weary. A child of about three came and snuggled up to her side. She fell into a peaceful sleep.

I knew then that she had given me her blessing to be the "grammie" she could not be to her unborn grandchildren. That first grandchild is expected this June, by Greg and Caytie. I can hardly wait.

The other day, the phone rang. Someone from the Gift of Life Center Northwest was on the phone. She called to tell me that the State of Washington awards six families per year for their loved one's gift of life. Would we want to participate and receive the award? She went on to explain the governor from our state would give an award to each family. What an honor and tribute to Blair! The fact that his two kidneys gave life to two men makes it easier to bear his loss. So on February 28, 2012, we will be there with five other families to accept the award. And Blair Graybill will be the most honored for it was his gift. I am so thankful that though this is an honor, his greatest honor is his life in heaven with his Lord and Savior.

As Greg said in a Sunday sermon, "Put God at the center of your life now, so that when everything else falls away—as it will—you will still possess the vital center."

He is the center of my life. He has provided. He is trustworthy and good.

Photos

Bill and Shirley at Glacier National Park

We're engaged!

Memorial Hike, 2008. Top of Hamilton Mountain

Blair and Shirley in Mountains of Colorado

Our Wedding

New Blended Family

First dance to "Fascination"

South Africa Safari

In South Africa

Mr. Robin

Glossary of Family Members
Blair Graybill and Shirley Rudberg married in 2008

Shirley's family

Shirley Mae Quiring married G. William Rudberg, Jr. on July 16, 1965
G. William Rudberg, Jr., 1943-2006

Children:

Todd Rudberg
Daughters, Rebekah and Sarah
Erika Rudberg Sagert married to Trent Sagert in 1995
Andrew, Caleb, Annabel and Emily (Also known as the "Tribe")

Shirley's Siblings

Joyce Erickson and husband Dick

Children:

Diana Erickson married to Lee Strucker
David Erickson
Jonathan Erickson married to Kelly

Roger Quiring and wife Lexie
Eileen Qutub and husband Abe

CHILDREN:

Michelle Lowry

CHILDREN:

Joseph
Betsy Berry and husband Lyle

CHILDREN:

Aaron Berry married to Kelly
Kirsten Hauan married to Jordan
Peter Berry

BLAIR GRAYBILL'S FAMILY

Married Patricia Venebles in 1972
Patricia "Wisha" Venebles Graybill 1946-2004

CHILDREN

Greg Graybill married to Caytie in 2005
Jonathan Graybill

BLAIR'S SIBLINGS

John Graybill married to Andy
Oscar "Digger" Graybill married to April

CHILDREN

Erin, Kevin
Jane Graybill

Glossary of Family Members

Blair's In-laws:

Tod and Mary Caroline Hunt- parents of Caytie
Dennis and Jennifer Adams- Patricia's sister and brother in law

Children

Kate deWaal

Children

Tanika
Vicky Adams Drinkwater married to Dave

Children

Richard, Katelyn

GEORGE WILLIAM RUDBERG, JR.

GEORGE WILLIAM (BILL) Rudberg, Jr. was born in Portland, Oregon on Sunday, September 26, 1943 to George and Marian Rudberg. He attended school at Alameda Elementary School. His family moved to Glendale, California where Bill attended and graduated from Garfield High School. During his high school years, he was in ROTC Drill Team and chess club.

In 1955, he accepted Christ as his personal Savior and was baptized soon after. In 1963, he returned to the NW and resided in Vancouver, Washington, and attended Clark College where he received his AAS degree in 1965.

He attended Brush Prairie Baptist Church where he met his wife Shirley. They resided in Vancouver most of their married life. Their first child, Todd William, was born on October 5, 1967. Daughter, Erika Ann, was born on June 27, 1973. Their third child, Carrie Lynn, was stillborn on June 13, 1977. Bill loved his children very much and as a family did much in the outdoors: camping, motorcycle riding, fishing, hunting, rock climbing and mountain climbing. Todd, Erika, and Shirley all summited Mount Hood led by Bill at separate times.

He experienced much joy with his grandchildren, Rebekah, Sarah, Andrew, Caleb, Annabel, and Emily. Much time and effort was spent with them. He regularly took the boys for their haircuts, camped with his older granddaughters, and gave all but the baby girls' airplane rides.

Bill was a man of many talents. He raced sports cars, rode motorcycles, was a commercial fisherman, a talented photographer, a mountaineer and rock climber leading many outings for a local mountaineering club and church members. Later Bill became interested in training retrievers and had a special relationship with his Lab, Card, his most loyal duck and goose hunting partner. Throughout his life he had a passion for aviation and in the late 1960's quickly built up many hours earning his private pilot license, commercial, IFR, multi-engine and CFII ratings. To top off his aviation career he and his son, Todd, built an exciting high performance sport plane which he enjoyed flying as far south as San Diego, California, and as far north as the Yukon Territories, north of the 60th parallel.

Bill was an influential man because he was liked by many and because he shared his interests with so many. Bill was the recreational director of the family and to his last day was planning the family's next event. He will be greatly missed by his wife, son, daughter, son-in-law, grandchildren, mother, and brother. He loved his Lord and Savior Jesus Christ and instead of being embittered by the physical pain and disability suffered at the end of his life, allowed the adversity to make this relationship stronger. As the discomforts of his illness grew worse, Bill quit complaining completely. We love you Bill.

Henry Blair Graybill II

HENRY BLAIR GRAYBILL II was born on November 12, 1944, to Harry and Martha Jane O'Connell Graybill in Clifton Forge, Virginia.

Blair grew up in Manhattan Beach, California, and graduated from Aviation High School in 1962 and San Jose State University in 1967. He served in the Peace Corps in Colombia, South America. He met his wife, Patricia on a trip to South Africa in 1972. They were married on December 23, 1972, and had two sons, Gregory and Jonathan.

Blair taught junior high school in Los Angeles, California, before moving to Walla Walla, Washington, in 1979. He taught English and Social Studies at Pioneer Junior High School and Walla Walla High School.

He loved history, especially the Civil War, and toured numerous battlefields. In 2000, Blair and Pat moved to Charlottesville, Virginia, where he served as a tour guide at Thomas Jefferson's home, Monticello, as well as President Monroe's residence, Ash-Lawn Highland.

In 2003, they moved to Vancouver, Washington, where he taught at Summit View High School in Battle Ground, Washington. Pat died of cancer in 2004.

In 2008, Blair met Shirley Rudberg, whose husband had died of complications from leukemia in 2006. Blair and Shirley immediately connected over faith, politics, and personality. After a whirlwind courtship, they were married on August 16, 2008, in Vancouver, Washington. They enjoyed spending time with family, hiking, ballroom dancing, and traveling.

Blair Graybill lived in faith in Jesus Christ and died trusting in Him for his salvation.

Surviving are his wife, Shirley, sons, Gregory(Cathryn) and Jonathan Graybill; daughter, Erika (Trent) Sagert and their four children, Andrew, Caleb, Annabel and Emily; son, Todd Rudberg and his two daughters, Rebekah and Sarah, brothers John (Andrienne) and Oscar (April) Graybill; and sister, Jane Graybill.

Mega-hike is a family memorial for fathers

Come 4 a.m. on Saturday, a small, hardy band of hikers will start up the steep Dog Mountain trail in the Columbia Gorge on the first leg of what they call the "Tri-Mountain Marathon."

They'll hustle up and down the popular, wildflower-studded peak in eastern Skamania County, then drive west and start up the even steeper Table Mountain trail near North Bonneville at 8 a.m.

At 1 p.m., they'll start up steep Hamilton Mountain trail in Beacon Rock State Park. By the end of the third leg, the group will have hiked 25 miles and climbed 8,000 feet of elevation.

But this is—only peripherally—a tale about hiking.

It's really a story about a family's way to honor the memories of their fathers on the day before Father's Day in a way the late Bill Rudberg and late Blair Graybill would have approved.

At the center of this is Shirley Graybill, 64, of Vancouver.

Shirley was married for 40 years to Bill Rudberg, who died of a stroke in February of 2006. A Columbia Machine employee, Rudberg loved to hike. Oh how did he love to hike!

It was Rudberg who, in 1994, concocted the idea of hiking the three steepest trails on the Washington side of the Gorge in a single day. Rudberg wore out a pair of hiking boots every 12 to 18 months.

Bill's son, Todd, began the Rudberg Memorial Hike [Shirley's note: Bruce Dishaw, a Columbia Machine employee and friend, started the memorial hikes, Todd re-invented his dad's tri-mountain marathon] in 2006 as an annual way for family and friends to remember the man by spending the day doing what he might have done.

Rudberg's widow, Shirley remarried, in August 2008. Her second husband, Blair Graybill, died suddenly of a brain aneurysm in January. He'd been a history teacher at Summit View High School, and in Walla Walla.

Graybill said on Father's Day, particularly, she thinks about what she's lost.

"And I grieve for my children, who don't have their dads and miss them," she said. "Now, I have two more boys."

Participating in Saturday's mega hike will be Bill Rudberg's son and daughter, plus two of his grandsons, ages nine and eleven. Joining them will be both sons of Blair Graybill, traveling here from Arizona and Pennsylvania.

Via the steep trails of the Gorge, this blended family will honor their husbands, fathers, and grandfathers.

Shirley Graybill is participating too.

While she'll skip the 4 A.M. ascent up Dog Mountain, she'll be on the trail at 8 A.M. for Table Mountain and 1 P.M. for Hamilton Mountain.

Anyone who's hiked this trio of trails knows any of the three in a day is plenty. Table Mountain, at one point, gains 800 feet elevation in one-third of a mile.

Both of her husbands, especially Rudberg, who lead (sic) group hikes for the Friends of the Columbia Gorge, would have encouraged anyone to come along.

"He learned skills, then he wanted to share them," Graybill said of Rudberg. "He did a lot of Friends of the Gorge hikes and was a definite leader."[13]

RECIPES

JOPIE'S DELIGHT

Serves 5 – 6

2 eggs separated

1 cup sugar

¼ cup cake flour

1 cup milk

1 T lemon juice

¾ cup orange juice

Grated rind of 1 lemon

2 T melted butter

Preheat oven to 180 degrees.

Beat the egg yolks, then fold in the sugar.

Add the flour and milk alternately.

Add the lemon juice, orange juice, grated rind and melted butter.

Beat the egg whites until stiff, then fold into the mixture.

Turn the batter into a greased fireproof baking dish, place in a pan of hot water and bake for 45 minutes or until nicely browned.

Milk Tart

Pastry:

¼ pound butter, melt. Add 1 heaped cup of flour.

Cook through.

Add 2 T icing sugar (fine grated sugar) and a good pinch of salt.

Press in pie dish and prick well. Bake 180 until golden brown.

Milk Tart Filling:

Makes 2 tarts

Four cups milk with one T butter-bring to a boil

1 cup sugar

3 level T cake flour

3 level T corn flour

2 eggs

Fix to a smooth paste

1 t vanilla

Add this mixture to the milk and butter, stirring constantly.

Cook for a few minutes until it thickens.

Add vanilla/or almond essence.

Pour in shells. Dust with cinnamon. Bake in hot oven. 425 for 30 minutes. This is delicious!

Dorothy's Banana Cake

2½ c. cake flour

1⅔ c sugar

1¼ t baking powder

1¼ t baking soda

1 t salt

⅔ c butter

⅔ c buttermilk

1¼ c mashed bananas

2 eggs

⅔ c chopped nuts

Sift dry ingredients

Add butter.

Mix with ⅓ c milk and bananas

Beat for two minutes

Add ⅓ c milk with eggs

Beat for two more minutes

Bake at 350 for 30-35 minutes in layered pans

45 minutes in a 9X13 pan

Icing

½ c butter

½ c shortening

1 c sugar

¾ c milk, warmed

1 t vanilla

Cream shortening and butter, add sugar, warm milk, add vanilla.

Babotie

(This is Wisha's recipe)

Soak one thick slice of bread in 1 ½ cups milk

Fry 1 large onion sliced in 1½ T butter or oil until transparent. Sprinkle 1½ T curry powder over it and cook through for a few minutes.

Add:

1 T vinegar

1 t Worcestershire Sauce

1 T apricot jam

1 T chutney

1 banana- sliced

½ c seeded raisins

2 t salt and ¼ t pepper

1 T sugar

Brown meat lightly (it can be ground beef, lamb, turkey, chicken).

Add drained bread which has been mixed with 1 beaten egg. Mix well and turn into a buttered pie dish.

Beat remaining egg and milk together and pour over meat in the dish.

Push Bay leaves into Babotie until just the stalks are showing.

Bake at 180 for 30 to 40 minutes. Pull out bay leaves before serving.

ROASTED RED PEPPER SOUP

Broil three large red bell peppers, turning as needed until completely charred, 10-12 minutes.

Cool; remove stems, seeds and skin and coarsely chop.

Peel and coarsely chop three medium Yukon Gold potatoes.

Cook one large chopped onion in olive oil until lightly browned. Add potatoes, peppers, and four cups vegetable or chicken broth.

Bring to a boil; then simmer, covered, until potatoes are tender when pierced, 10-15 minutes.

Puree soup in a blender in batches. Reheat in pan, thinning with more broth if you like. Season with salt.

Top it with a drizzle of olive oil. Serves 4-6.

KRULLERS

2 eggs

1 cup sour cream

1 t. baking soda

½ t. salt

2 T. sugar

1½ c flour (self-rising flour works well)

hot oil for deep frying

Mix eggs and sour cream. Add baking soda, salt, sugar & flour. Dough will be soft, but if too soft, add more flour.

Roll dough into rectangular pieces approximately 5 inches long. Place a slit in the middle so that the oil will flow through the center and cook well.

Test the oil with a small piece of dough to see if it is ready. Then, use a spatula to pick up the rectangular pieces from the board. Toss each piece back and forth in both hands to shake off the excess flour before placing in hot oil.

Cook until golden brown & place on paper towels to drain.

Serve with cool, sweet watermelon.

ENDNOTES

1. Thomas A. Dorsey, (1938 by Hill & Range Songs, Inc.).
2. Emilie Barnes, *Fill My Cup, Lord* (1996 by Harvest House Publishers, Eugene, Oregon).
3. "Fascination," TEXT, Maurice de Feaudy, 1905 (English lyrics Dick Manning) MUSIC, Fermo Dante Marchetti, 1904.
4. "You're My Thrill" Jay Gorney, lyrics by Sidney Clare, 1933.
5. "I've Dreamed of You" lyrics Warner/Chappell Music, Inc., Universal Music Publishing Group.
6. "What a Wonderful World." Bob Thiele and George David Weiss, 1967.
7. Charles Major, *The Bears of Blue River* (The Library of Indian Classics, 1984).
8. Joseph Bayly, *The Last Thing We Talk About: Help and Hope for Those Who Grieve*. David C. Cook, Elgin Illinois, 1969.
9. Gregory B. Graybill, *Evangelical Free Will Philipp Melanchthon's Doctrinal Journey on the Origins of Faith* (Oxford University Press, 2010).
10. "Part the Waters, Lord." Words and music by Charles F. Brown. Word Music, 1975.

11. "Amazing Grace," John Newton. Public domain.
12. Samuel Rodigast (1675), tr. Catherine Winkworth (1863. a;t/ 1961).
13. Al Thomas, *The Columbian*. June 17, 2010.

WinePressPublishing
Great Books, Defined.

To order additional copies of this book call:
1-877-421-READ (7323)
or please visit our website at
www.WinePressbooks.com

If you enjoyed this quality custom-published book,
drop by our website for more books and information.

www.winepresspublishing.com

"Your partner in custom publishing."